ENGLISH 12/13

English 12/13

R. S. Fowler and A. J. B. Dick

London
GEORGE ALLEN & UNWIN LTD
RUSKIN HOUSE . MUSEUM STREET

First published 1972

© George Allen & Unwin Ltd 1972

ISBN 0 04 428030 0

Text set in 11/12 pt. Monotype Baskerville, printed by photolithography, and bound in Great Britain at The Pitman Press, Bath

Contents

Acknowledgements

We are grateful for the resources provided by Sittingbourne College of Education and its library. We are particularly grateful to Eileen Greenwood, the Principal.

We should also like to thank David Male for his advice on Improvisation.

Above all, for their unlimited help and encouragement, we thank our wives Penelope and Virginia, and our editor, Tony Wilson.

We are also grateful to the following authors, publishers and agents for permission to reprint copyright material from the works mentioned below:

The Bodley Head (Rosemary Sutcliff's *The High Deeds of Finn Mac Cool*); Mrs M. Thomas (3 poems from Edward Thomas's *Collected Poems*); Penguin Books Ltd (Edward Blishen (ed.) and contributors' *The School that I'd Like*); Chatto, Boyd & Oliver (John Hornby's *Clowns through the Ages*); Faber & Faber Ltd (M. R. James's translation of *Hans Andersen: Forty-two Stories*); The Reverend David Mowbray ('Musician's Lament'); Hutchinson Publishing Group Ltd (John Arden's *Here Today*); J. M. Dent & Sons Ltd and the Trustees for the Copyright of the late Dylan Thomas (Dylan Thomas's *Portrait of the Artist as a Young Dog*); George Allen & Unwin Ltd (J. R. R. Tolkien's *The Lord of the Rings*); Curtis Brown Ltd (N. F. Simpson's *One Way Pendulum*); Lawrence Pollinger Ltd and Cresset Press (Carson McCullers's *The Member of The Wedding*); Lawrence Pollinger Ltd, William Heinemann Ltd, and the Estate of the late Mrs Frieda Lawrence (D. H. Lawrence's *The Rainbow* and *The Complete Poems of D. H. Lawrence*); Jonathan Cape Ltd and the Estates of Kenneth Walker and Geoffrey Boumphrey (Kenneth Walker and Geoffrey Boumphrey's *The Log of the Ark*); David Higham Associates Ltd (John Heath-Stubbs's 'The History of the Flood', from *A Charm against the Toothache*); Collins (Alan Garner's *The Weirdstone of Brisingamen*); Michael Joseph Ltd (Barry Hines's *A Kestrel for a Knave*); Chatto & Windus Ltd (Iris Murdoch's *The Flight from the Enchanter*); Hamish Hamilton Ltd (Nancy Mitford's *The Pursuit of Love*); Faber & Faber Ltd (Ted Hughes's *Meet My Folks!*); Jonathan Cape Ltd (Liam O'Flaherty's *Short Story*); Chatto & Windus Ltd and Mr George Scott Moncrieff (Marcel Proust's *Swann's Way*, translated by C. K. Scott Moncrieff); The Harvill Press Ltd (K. Paustovsky's *Story of a Life*, translated by Manya Harari and Michael Duncan); Hughes Massie Ltd (Paul Gallico's *Love of Seven Dolls*); Oxford and Cambridge University Presses (*New English Bible*); W. H. Allen Ltd and Rosica Colin Ltd (Alan Sillitoe's *The Loneliness of the*

Long Distance Runner); The Society of Authors as the literary representatives of the Estate of Katherine Mansfield (Katherine Mansfield's *The Garden Party and Other Stories*); ACTAC (Theatrical and Cinematic) Ltd (David Campton's *The Lunatic View*); The Bodley Head (Paul Berna's *A Hundred Million Francs*, translated by John Buchanan-Brown); Faber & Faber Ltd (Ted Hughes's *Wodwo*); Mr James MacGibbon as executor for Stevie Smith (Stevie Smith's 'Harold's Leap', from *Short Story*); Faber & Faber Ltd (T. S. Eliot's *Old Possum's Book of Practical Cats*); Essex Music Ltd (Lee Hays's and Pete Seeger's song 'If I had a Hammer'); the *Daily Mirror* Children's Literary Competition (Angela Stratton's 'My Life Story').

We are grateful also to the photographers whose work is reproduced and credited in the book; to the Headmaster of Coopers Lane Primary School, London S.E.12, for permission to use the photograph on page 108; to Dr Bernhard Grzimek for the pictures on pages 170–171, reproduced from his book *Amongst the Animals of Africa* (Collins); and to Frau T. Dürst-Haass of Muttenz for the cover illustration of Paul Klee's *Sinbad the Sailor*.

9

Index of Authors

About the Book

Language Work

We have tried to provide for all kinds of language work: for writing, reading and talking. We have not on the whole provided conventional language exercises because they tend to be artificial, out of context or not, and rarely deal satisfactorily with individual problems; and also because they would get in the way of more useful work on the material. We believe that the best way to correct and improve a pupil's use of English is to provide the kind of environment in which he will be concerned with what he is writing and saying; after that it is up to the teacher to correct work individually, or with the class as a whole where there are common problems.

Pictures

These are not generally illustrations of the text, although they often add a comment to a theme under discussion. Work is suggested in relation to the pictures, but it is expected that teachers and pupils will also have their own ideas about how they will look at the illustrations.

A book of this kind has to make do of course with a small selection of pictures. The introduction by teacher and pupils of other pictures, from magazines, newspapers and libraries, for example, is one of the ways by which the work suggested in the book can be extended and enriched.

Films, Music and Books

Apart from some suggestions in the text, there are no lists included. The introduction by teachers and pupils of their own suggestions will increase the scope of the course. Pupils and teacher might find it useful to compile their own lists of 'books worth reading', 'films worth seeing', and 'music worth hearing'.

Extracts, Poems and Questions

Some of the extracts and poems are clearly much more difficult than others, but the questions themselves often elucidate the more difficult pieces, and it is expected that teachers and pupils will use the book in the way that benefits their particular situation most.

Pupils who find particular difficulty might nevertheless benefit from an oral treatment of the material in class after the first reading.

Beowulf

The extracts and poems are structured round a version of the eighth-century poem *Beowulf*. The version is formal as that Old English poem is formal. It aims to preserve a distant vision of a hero and a heroic past, in a story which illustrates a universal question: how am I to behave in this mysterious world?

R. S. FOWLER
A. J. B. DICK

I (1) Of strange comings and goings

1. '*Who are you? What is your name?*
   Where is it that you come from?'

2. *Will you come?*

3. '*I am a man, upon the land,*
   I am a silkie in the sea;
   And when I'm far and far from land,
   My dwelling is in Sule Skerrie.'

4. '*There dwells a loved one,*
   But cruel is she!
   She left lonely for ever
   The kings of the sea.'

5. *Grendel, of the tribe of Cain!*

'Who are you? What is your name?'

Finn Mac Cool was captain of the Fianna, a war-band who guarded ancient Ireland's shores against attack and kept peace within the country. He owned two great hounds, Bran and Skolawn.

Finn and his companions rode hunting in their home woods, and as they returned at evening towards Almu of the White Walls, suddenly a young dappled hind sprang up from the fern and foxgloves of a little clearing, almost under the nose of Finn's horse, and bounded away into the trees.

Finn's companions set up a great burst of hunting cries, and slipped the hounds from leash, and the hounds, weary as they were, sprang away on the track of the fleeing hind, and instantly the whole hunt swept after them, all the weariness of the day forgotten in the music of the hounds and the rush of the horses' speed and the excitement of the new chase.

But Finn noticed a strange thing, that however much the hind doubled and twisted in her track, she was drawing steadily nearer to the Hill of Almu itself. Almost it seemed as though she were trying to reach the place, like one running for sanctuary, yet what sanctuary could a hunted hind look for in the dun of the hunter?

On they sped, the hind well ahead, seen and lost among the trees, the hounds streaking on her trail, the horsemen thundering after. But the hind was as swift as a cloud shadow on a March day, and soon only Finn himself and his two great hounds still had her in sight, while the rest of the hunt fell farther behind, and at last all sound of them was lost in the wind-rustle and bee-drone and cuckoo-call of the summer woods.

Once, the hind checked her speed and glanced back, as though to see who rode close on her trail, then fled on again, with Bran and Skolawn close behind her.

For a few moments the three were lost to view, where the alder and hazel and quicken trees clustered thick along the fringes of the forest, and then, as he crashed out through the undergrowth on to the open moors that surrounded the Hill of Almu, Finn came upon the strangest sight that ever he had seen. For there in a little hollow set about with fern and shadowy with harebells, the hind lay panting from her long run, and Bran and Skolawn were standing over her, licking her face and her trembling limbs as though to tell her that she was safe with them and had nothing now to fear.

And while Finn stood staring, and the hind turned her graceful head and looked at him with the soft long-lashed eyes of her tribe, he heard the Fian hunting horn, and then the music of the hounds close at hand.

The hind sprang to her feet and stood trembling, and instantly Bran and Skolawn set themselves on either side of her, their hackles rising as they prepared if need be to fight. Then Finn wheeled his horse across the path of the hunt as they came up, and shouted to the Fianna to call off their hounds.

The horsemen reined in, pulling the horses back on their haunches, and seeing what was behind their Captain, called off their hounds in a hurry, for they knew Bran and Skolawn when their hackles rose like that, and knew that any hound who took up their challenge would be a hound lost to the pack. But Goll Mac Morna looked at the trembling hind and said, 'This is surely a strange quarry that you have run to bay.'

'It is in my mind that she was striving to reach Almu,' Finn said, half laughing at the foolishness of his own thought, yet holding to it all the same, 'and a poor thing it would be if a man were to hunt the guest who seeks his gates.'

So the hunting party rode on, across the level country and up the Hill of Almu. And sure enough, the hind went ahead of them, and she playing with Bran and Skolawn by the way. And when they came to the gates, in she went, and that evening at supper she lay at Finn's feet, with the two great hounds one on either side of her.

In the midst of that night, Finn woke with a start. His sleeping hut was white with moonlight that flooded in through the open door, and standing in the heart of the moonlight, like the gold in the heart of a white flower, was the most beautiful maiden that ever his eyes had touched upon. She wore a gown of soft saffron wool clasped at the shoulder with yellow gold, and out of it her neck rose white, and her slim bare arms were white, and her hair was so warmly golden that even the moon could not wash the gold out of it. Only her eyes were soft and dark and shadowed with long black lashes as the eyes of the hind had been.

'Who are you?' said Finn, wonderingly.

'If you wish for a name to call me by, then call me Saba,' said the maiden. 'I am the hind that you hunted today.'

'This is beyond my understanding,' said Finn, rubbing his hand across his forehead. 'Am I dreaming? If so, I hope it's a dream I'll be remembering in the morning.'

'You are not dreaming,' the maiden said. 'Listen, and you shall understand. Three of your mortal years ago, the Dark Druid of my own people tried to force his love on me and have me for his wife, and because I would have none of him, he used his magic to put upon me the hind's shape that I have worn ever since. But a slave of his who took pity on me and had good cause to hate him, told me that if once I could win to the Dun of Almu, within the white walls of Finn Mac Cool, I should be safe from the spells of our dark master, and my true shape would come to me again. Today I found the chance to let myself be run down by you and no other hunter, and by your dogs Bran and Skolawn, who have enchantment in them also, and the hearts of men, and who would know me for what I am and do me no harm.'

'Here you are safe indeed,' Finn said, 'and none shall harm you or seek to force his love on you nor bind you with any bond against your will. But can you be happy among mortal folk, and you with never one of your kind to speak with or to touch your hand?'

For he knew that her own people of whom she spoke were the Fairy Kind.

Saba said, 'I can be happy anywhere in the Three Worlds with you, and not happy anywhere without you. You have done that to me, you who promised that in Almu no one should bind me with any bond against my will.'

So she became Finn's wife, and their happiness was like the happiness of the Immortals in the Land of Youth where spring never turns to winter, and magic birds sing always in the branches of the white apple trees whose blossom never falls, even when the apples sweeten and turn gold.

The months went by, and they wanted nothing in the world but to be in each other's company. Indeed, as moon followed moon, and summer turned to autumn and autumn to winter and back to spring, and Finn seemed to have no taste left for war or hunting or anything that could take him from her side, the Fianna began to mutter among themselves that their Captain was not the man he had been before her coming.

17

And then one day word came to Almu of the White Walls that there were Lochlan war-boats in Dublin Bay.

Then Finn roused himself, and called out the Fianna of the Five Provinces. And in the forecourt of Almu, as in other strongholds through the length and breadth of Erin, the warriors gathered to sharpen sword and spear blade on the tall weapon stone.

Saba seemed to grow whiter and thinner as she watched, and once she said to Finn with her arms round his neck, 'Need you go?'

But Finn replied: 'A man lives after his life, but not after his honour', and gently pulled her arms from about his neck, and went out to see how the armourers were doing.

At the very last, with the warriors waiting before the gates, he said, 'Wait for me, bird-of-my-heart, and soon we shall be together again. But while I am away, promise me that you will not set foot outside the walls of Almu, nor speak to anyone not of our household.'

And Saba promised, and Finn marched away. . . .

With every step of the homeward way, Finn thought more strongly of Saba, and his heart went out ahead of him to be with her again. And when they reached the foot of the Hill of Almu and began to climb, his gaze went searching to and fro along the ramparts and among all the possible look-out places, for the first sight of her waiting for him. But no sign of Saba could he see. And when he came into the forecourt and looked about him, thinking that now surely she would come running, still there was no sign of her, not so much as the glimmer of a single golden hair. And his household hung back, with trouble in their faces, instead of crowding forward to greet him as they usually did, and seemed to find it hard to meet his eyes.

And suddenly a cold hand seemed to close on Finn's heart.

'Where is the Lady Saba?' he demanded. 'Is she sick? Why is she not here to greet me?'

Then his steward came forward with bent head, and told him what he asked.

'While you were away, Lord of Almu, aye, not three days since, we saw one coming up the hill towards the gate, who seemed in all things so far as the eye could tell to be yourself, and with him two hounds who had the outward seeming of Bran and Skolawn, even to the three black hairs on the tip of Skolawn's tail. And at the same time we seemed to hear the sound of the

Fian hunting horn. Then the Lady Saba, who was watching from the gatehouse roof, as she had watched all and every day for your return, cried out glad and sweet, and hurried down to where the men were already opening the gate for your coming in. We shouted to her to remain within, but truly, it is in my mind that she never heard us, and she was out through the gate like the dart of a swallow, and running down the hill.'

'And then?' said Finn in a terrible voice.

'When she came close to him who wore your shape and seeming, she checked, and gave a loud, bitter cry, and turned to run back towards the gate. But he struck her with a hazel wand, and there, where she had been, was a dappled hind, and she doubling and twisting piteously as still she tried to reach the gate, and the two hounds drove her back. We seized our weapons and ran out to aid her, but when we reached the place, there was nothing to be seen. Neither hind nor hounds nor enchanter, not so much as their shadows on the bare hillside. And suddenly the air was filled with a great rushing, shouts and cries and the hoof-drum of galloping horses and the baying of hounds, and some of us thought that it came from this direction, and some that it came from that, until at last all died away into the wind. We have searched all the country round, but there is no trace of her nor of those who hunted her. Oh, my Lord Finn, the Lady Saba is lost to us!'

From coast to coast of Erin Finn sought her. But nowhere did he find any trace of her.

And when seven years were past, he gave up all hope of finding her again, and began to hunt with the rest of the Fianna as of old.

One day they were hunting on Ben Bulben in Sligo, the hounds running far ahead, when he heard their trail-music change to a fierce yelping and snarling like a dog fight. He and his companions ran forward—they were hunting on foot that day, for the mountain runs were too steep for the ponies—and found a naked boy standing under a quicken tree, the hounds striving to seize him, all save Bran and Skolawn, who with fangs bared and ears laid back, had sprung forward and turned on the rest of the pack to hold them off.

Memory smote Finn under the heart, and he remembered another time that he had come upon his two great hounds doing this very thing. But then it had been to protect a dappled hind. . . .

His men gathered round, beating off the hounds, while the boy stood quite unafraid, looking round from one to another of them. He was tall and well shaped, though slight of build—a runner rather than a wrestler, thought Finn, who was used to judging in these matters—and his hair was almost as pale as Finn's own, so that his dark eyes seemed all the more dark by contrast. He stood like a wild thing, tensed and light on his feet, yet still proudly unafraid.

'Who are you?' Finn said.

The boy looked at him, but spoke no word.

'What is your name? Where is it that you come from?'

Still the boy said no word, and suddenly Keelta Mac Ronan said, 'It is no good to ask him. Don't you see? He knows only the Wild. He does not understand man's tongue!'

So Finn held out his open hand to the boy, slowly and re-assuringly, so that he might understand there was no menace in it. The boy looked from his face to his outstretched hand and back again. 'Come,' said Finn, as he might have said to a hound puppy he was training, knowing that the pup would not yet know the meaning of the word, but his voice speaking it would mean something all the same. And slowly, the boy came and set his hand in Finn's.

So they returned to Almu with the strange boy in their midst. And all the way, Finn watched him, as though some great question was in his mind, and the boy was the answer.

At first he was like a wild creature caged. But at last, hesitating and stumbling at the outset, he began to gain the power of human speech.

And when speech came easily enough to him for story telling, it was a strange story he had to tell Finn.

Ever since he could remember, he had lived with a dappled hind. He supposed that she was his mother, for he had had no other, nor any father, so far as he knew. And she had given him milk when he was very small, and the warmth of her own body curled about him when the nights were cold, and comfort when he was hurt or unhappy, and love and gentleness at all times. They had lived in a green and beautiful valley, from which—he was not quite sure how or why—there seemed no way out, but he supposed there must have been, after all, because assuredly there was a way in, though he had never found it. And this he knew, because though he lived on nuts and berries in summer, in

winter food was left for him daily in a certain cave on the hillside; and also because a man came to them at times, a very tall dark man, at whose coming he had always been troubled and afraid. Sometimes the man spoke to the hind his mother in tones that were darkly sweet as heather honey, sometimes in a voice hard with menace, but always the hind shrank away and would not even look at him; until at last he went off again, very angry.

And then there came a day when the dark stranger spoke with his mother for a very long time, sometimes pleadingly and gently, sometimes urgently and as though there were pain within him, sometimes ragingly, like a cold gale through the woods in winter, but still she would do nothing but shrink away from him, yet keeping always between him and the boy. At last the man gave up pleading and threatening alike, and did a thing that the boy had never seen him do before. He lifted up the hazel wand which he always carried in his hand and struck her with it, and then turned instantly and strode away.

And this time the hind followed him, trembling and seeming as though she strove to draw back, but following still.

Then the boy was terribly afraid, and cried out to his mother not to leave him. But when he would have run after her, his feet seemed to have taken root in the ground. And his mother looked back at him, piteously, the great tears falling from her eyes. Yet still she followed the dark man as though he drew her after him on a chain.

Then, still struggling to follow her, crying out in rage and terror and desolation, the boy fell to the ground, and into a blackness that was like sleep but not like good sleep.

When he awoke from the blackness, he was lying on the bare heather slopes of Ben Bulben. And he was alone.

For days he hung about the slopes of the mountain, seeking and seeking for his hidden valley, and never finding it again, until at last the Fian hunting dogs found him.

So Finn knew that he would never find Saba again, but he knew also that she had left him a son.

He called the boy Oisīn, which means Little Fawn.

But the story of Saba and the Dark Druid he could not give an end to. No one knows the end of that story, to this day.

ROSEMARY SUTCLIFF: 'The Birth of Oisīn' from
The High Deeds of Finn Mac Cool

Questions

What was strange in the behaviour of the hind and Finn's hounds?

What is *sanctuary*?

Why did the hind make for the Hill of Almu?

Why did Finn have to leave Saba?

What promise to Finn did Saba break?

How was Saba deceived into breaking her promise?

What difficulty did the strange boy have when Finn took him to his home?

If the boy could have understood the words, what do you think he would have heard the Dark Druid saying to Saba, and what do you think were her replies?

From the information in the extract, describe in your own words how Finn and Saba met. You need not keep just to the information in the extract. You may do as Rosemary Sutcliff says she does—add 'a flicker or a flourish' of your own from time to time.

Discussion

Should Finn have married Saba?

Should Finn have stayed with Saba after he had married her, or did he do right to lead the Fianna into battle? (Do you think he would have gone if he had known what was going to happen?)

Should soldiers get married?

Writing

Write a story called 'The Return of Saba'.

Project

Make a collection of the stories of Finn Mac Cool or of other great legends.

Reading

The High Deeds of Finn Mac Cool by Rosemary Sutcliff (Bodley Head).

Will You Come?

Will you come?
Will you come?
Will you ride
So late
At my side?
O, will you come?

Will you come?
Will you come
If the night
Has a moon,
Full and bright?
O, will you come?

Would you come?
Would you come
If the noon
Gave light,
Not the moon?
Beautiful, would you come?

Would you have come?
Would you have come
Without scorning,
Had it been
Still morning?
Beloved, would you have come?

If you come
Haste and come.
Owls have cried;
It grows dark
To ride.
Beloved, beautiful, come.

EDWARD THOMAS

Write an answer to this poem.

'I am a man, upon the land,
I am a silkie in the sea'

The previous story told of a mortal man who married a fairy bride. This
ballad tells of the Great Silkie of Sule Skerrie. Silkies were also creatures
of enchantment, who sometimes changed their seal skins to appear on land
in human guise. There they chose a mortal wife to bring up their children.

The Great Silkie of Sule Skerrie

An earthly nurse sits and sings
And aye she sings, sleep little one!
I do not know my bairn's father
Far less the land that he dwells in.

Then one arose at her bed feet
And a grumly guest I'm sure was he,
'Here am I, thy bairn's father
Although I be not comely.

'I am a man, upon the land,
I am a silkie on the sea;
And when I'm far and far from land,
My dwelling is in Sule Skerrie.'

'It was not good,' said the maiden fair,
'It was not good, indeed,' said she,
'That the Great Silkie of Sule Skerrie
Should have come and left his bairn with me.'

Now he has taken a purse of gold,
And he has put it upon her knee,
Saying 'Give to me my little young son,
And take thee up thy nurse's fee.

'And it shall come to pass on a summer's day,
When the sun shines hot on every stone,
That I will take my little young son,
And teach him how to swim the foam.

And you shall marry a proud gunner,
And a proud gunner I'm sure he'll be,
And the very first shot that ever he shoots,
He'll shoot both my young son and me.'

ANON.

Questions
Why is the Silkie making this visit to the mortal woman?
What future does the Silkie prophesy for the mortal?
What future does the Silkie prophesy for himself?

Discussion
Do ballads like this have any *use*? (Are there any lessons in
them? Do you believe any of them? Do you believe in mermaids? Do you believe in the Loch Ness Monster? Why do these
stories survive?)

Writing
In some versions of this ballad, further verses tell how the
Silkie's prophecy about himself and his son comes to pass.
Write some verses of your own, describing these events.

Project
Find out what you can about the Loch Ness Monster.
Write a history of mermaids.
If you enjoy ballads, you might like to look up some more of
them in *English and Scottish Popular Ballads*, collected by F. J.
Child. 'The Great Silkie' is ballad 113 in this collection.

Record
Joan Baez sings 'Silkie' on Fontana record STFL 6025. This is
a full-size stereo record. You may well be able to find the ballad
on a smaller record if you look in the catalogues.

Sunday Times

Give this picture a title.
Write a story or an account of your thoughts and feelings as you look at the picture.

Make a collection of unusual pictures, from several countries, including your own. When you have made your collection, write an introduction to the pictures. (What themes might you choose to link them? What illustrations which might seem quite usual in your own country will perhaps seem strange when viewed by people with different traditions, habits and customs?)

'There dwells a loved one,
But cruel is she!'

This poem tells the story of a Merman who marries a mortal bride. They have children and live happily together in the sea caverns, until one day Margaret, the Merman's wife, leaves him and does not return. At the beginning of the poem the Merman has gone to the shore with their children, and is calling after his wife. He then tells how it was that Margaret came to leave them.

The Forsaken Merman

Come, dear children, let us away;
Down and away below!
Now my brothers call from the bay,
Now the great winds shoreward blow,
Now the salt tides seaward flow;
Now the wild white horses play,
Champ and chafe and toss in the spray.
Children dear, let us away!
This way, this way!

Call her once before you go –
Call once yet!
In a voice that she will know:
'Margaret! Margaret!'
Children's voices should be dear
(Call once more) to a mother's ear;
Children's voices, wild with pain –
Surely she will come again!
Call her once and come away;
This way, this way!
'Mother dear, we cannot stay!
The wild white horses foam and fret.'
Margaret! Margaret!

Come, dear children, come away down;
Call no more!
One last look at the white-wall'd town,

And the little grey church on the windy shore,
Then come down!
She will not come though you call all day;
Come away, come away!
Children dear, was it yesterday
We heard the sweet bells over the bay?
In the caverns where we lay,
Through the surf and through the swell,
The far-off sound of a silver bell?
Sand-strewn caverns, cool and deep,
Where the winds are all asleep;
Where the spent lights quiver and gleam,
Where the salt weed sways in the stream,
Where the sea-beasts, ranged all round,
Feed in the ooze of their pasture-ground;
Where the sea-snakes coil and twine,
Dry their mail and bask in the brine;
Where great whales come sailing by,
Sail and sail, with unshut eye,
Round the world for ever and aye?
When did music come this way?
Children dear, was it yesterday?

Children dear, was it yesterday
(Call yet once) that she went away?
Once she sate with you and me,
On a red gold throne in the heart of the sea,
And the youngest sate on her knee.
She comb'd its bright hair, and she tended it well,
When down swung the sound of a far-off bell.
She sigh'd; she look'd up through the clear green sea;
She said: 'I must go, for my kinsfolk pray
In the little grey church on the shore today.
'Twill be Easter-time in the world – ah me!
And I lose my poor soul, Merman! here with thee.'
I said: 'Go up, dear heart, through the waves;
Say thy prayer, and come back to the kind sea-caves!'
She smiled, she went up through the surf in the bay.
Children dear, was it yesterday?

Children dear, were we long alone?
'The sea grows stormy, the little ones moan;

Long prayers,' I said, 'in the world they say;
Come!' I said; and we rose through the surf in the bay.
We went up the beach, by the sandy down
Where the sea-stocks bloom, to the white-wall'd town;
Through the narrow paved streets, where all was still,
To the little grey church on the windy hill.
From the church came a murmur of folk at their
    prayers,
But we stood without[1] in the cold blowing airs.
We climb'd on the graves, on the stones worn with rains,
And we gazed up the aisle through the small leaded panes.
She sate by the pillar; we saw her clear:
'Margaret, hist! come quick, we are here!
Dear heart,' I said, 'we are long alone;
The sea grows stormy, the little ones moan.'
But, ah, she gave me never a look,
For her eyes were seal'd to the holy book!
Loud prays the priest; shut stands the door.
Come away, children, call no more!
Come away, come down, call no more!

Down, down, down!
Down to the depths of the sea!
She sits at her wheel in the humming town,
Singing most joyfully.
Hark what she sings: 'O joy, O joy,
For the humming street, and the child with its toy!
For the priest, and the bell, and the holy well;
For the wheel where I spun,
And the blessed light of the sun!'
And so she sings her fill,
Singing most joyfully,
Till the spindle drops from her hand,
And the whizzing wheel stands still.
She steals to the window, and looks at the sand,
And over the sand at the sea;
And her eyes are set in a stare;
And anon there breaks a sigh,
And anon there drops a tear,

[1] Outside.

From a sorrow-clouded eye,
And a heart sorrow-laden,
A long, long sigh;
For the cold strange eyes of a little Mermaiden
And the gleam of her golden hair.

Come away, away children;
Come children, come down!
The hoarse wind blows coldly;
Lights shine in the town.
She will start from her slumber
When gusts shake the door;
She will hear the winds howling,
Will hear the waves roar.
We shall see, while above us
The waves roar and whirl,
A ceiling of amber,
A pavement of pearl.
Singing: 'Here came a mortal,
But faithless was she!
And alone dwell for ever
The kings of the sea.'

But, children, at midnight,
When soft the winds blow,
When clear falls the moonlight,
When spring-tides are low;
When sweet airs come seaward
From heaths starr'd with broom,
And high rocks throw mildly
On the blanch'd sands a gloom;
Up the still, glistening beaches,
Up the creeks we will hie,
Over banks of bright seaweed
The ebb-tide leaves dry.
We will gaze, from the sand-hills,
At the white, sleeping town;
At the church on the hill-side –
And then come back down.
Singing: 'There dwells a loved one,

But cruel is she!
She left lonely for ever
The kings of the sea.'

MATTHEW ARNOLD

Questions
Why did Margaret leave the Merman?
Why, do you think, did she not return to him?
Was she happy after she had left?

From the information in the extract, describe the Merman's home.

Discussion
Should Margaret have left her Merman husband and her children?

Writing
Write some further verses to this poem, describing the return of Margaret.

Improvisation
Create the underwater scene which is described in this poem.
(How could you suggest the movement of the sea, the salt weed, the sea-beasts and the sea-snakes? Observe how sea-weed and the sand move below the water with the movement of the tide.)
Use the music from *The Submerged Cathedral* by Debussy to provide a background to your scene.

Grendel, of the Tribe of Cain

Beowulf—1

Introduction: the minstrel begins his story by arresting the attention of his audience, and reminding them of the ancient glory of the Spear-Danes.

Hearken! while I commence my tale of Beowulf and his ancestors. First I tell of Scefing, the Shield-King, who was a foundling child saved from the sea, with only a sheaf of corn beside him in the empty boat. He grew to terrify his country's enemies and built his reputation by robbing his foes of their precious gift-thrones. He was a good king to his own people! His great achievements made up for his unhappy start in life.

Scefing the Shield-King was also blessed with a brave son, whom God granted to the warrior as a companion. This young prince prospered, and by his good deeds and generous gift-giving soon won many allies to support him against hostile armies. Let this be a lesson that by loving deeds any man may live happily amongst any people.

At last the time came for Scefing the Shield-King to leave this life to journey to the King of all mankind. His close friends in life bore him to the water's edge, just as he had requested while his words held sway. There, at the harbour, stood the royal barge, rime-frosted and ready to depart, ferrier of princes to far-off places. They laid their beloved Shield-King, giver of gifts, gently down by the mast in the bosom of the barge. With him were heaped piles of treasure, riches from far-off lands. Never have I heard of a vessel more handsomely furbished, fully fitted out with battle vestments and the trappings of war, filled with swords and superb shields. On the shield-bearer's breast lay a riot of riches, which were to sail with him far over the distant sea. They surrounded their Shield-King with treasures to equal those that had accompanied him when he was launched on the sea alone, a waif at the mercy of the lapping waves. Finally they fixed high over his head his standard of gold, then unloosed the barge and sent it slipping out to sea, giving him again to the waves. Their minds were mournful and their spirits sad. Neither prince nor ploughboy could tell for sure who took that Shield-King and his cargo to their final shelter.

The minstrel tells of the descendants of Scefing the Shield-King, and particularly of one Hrothgar, who built a mighty hall but did not enjoy it in safety for long:

With the departure of Scefing the Shield-King, his son and heir grew renowned in his kingdom. Then the Prince known as the Half-Dane was born and he succeeded to rule the Shield-King's people to a brave old age. Half-Dane had four children, one of whom was Hrothgar, with whom my tale begins.

Hrothgar had great success in battle, so that he won a willing throng of friendly warriors, who grew to be a mighty band of men. Hrothgar decided to build a mighty mead hall, a palace greater than the world had ever known, where he could freely give to young and old all that God had granted him. Then orders were given all over the world for the work to commence. Finally the day dawned when this greatest of feast halls was finished. Hrothgar, the King of poets, whose words had world-wide power, christened the hall 'Heorot'. He kept his word, and dealt out at great dinners an abundance of treasures.

The high flying roofs reached to the heavens. But the time would come when a deadly family feud would destroy the hall with fire.

At this time a dread demon who dwelt in the black depths of another world sweated in spiteful anger, for he could not bear to hear the revelry which echoed forth each day from the happy hall. The building used to ring with the strumming of the harp and the clear song of the minstrel.

He would recount from the most far off days the making of men, relate how the Almighty had made the earth a golden land encircled by the seas, and happy in his power had set the sun and the moon high in the sky to light up his work for his faithful folk below. He gave glory to the land with rich leaves and foliage, and life also he granted to every living thing.

Thus Hrothgar's warriors lived happily until the monster from the depths of hell began to work his wickednesses.

Grendel was the name of this ghastly, gruesome one, this beast of the borderlands, who reigned in terror over the tracts of fen and fastness. With all things evil he found his place, damned by

33

the Redeemer who avenged the killing of Abel on all Cain's kindred. Grendel was of the tribe of Cain, who was banished to outer darkness for his crime, whence were bred all evil errors, ogres and ylfes and orcs, and the gigantas, who for a long time waged war with God.

The minstrel goes on to tell how Grendel showed his hand:

When night had fallen Grendel took himself off to the elegant hall, to spy out how the warriors had bedded down after their banquet. He discovered therein a posse of princes dead to the world after their deep drinking. They were unsuspecting. In a trice of terror the mean unhallowed monster, disgruntled and greedy, ravaged thirty thanes where they lay. Then, mightily pleased with his grim mutilations, Grendel sought out his den, his dreadful appetite sated.

But by breakfast light Grendel's savage deed was seen by the soldiers, and a woeful cry racked the heavens. Hrothgar, desperately distracted, slumped on his throne. Downcast and dejected he suffered for his princes.

Nor was there breathing space, but night after night Grendel stepped up his deadly performances, fearsome and fatal and without mortal feelings; he was too deep in the blood of brave men. Soon it was easiest to find the men bestowed more safely, at a distance, in the adjoining buildings. Now the horrific hatred of the invader of Heorot was made terrifyingly clear to all by his mounting murders. To escape the monster the people hid at a safer distance. Thus Grendel held sway, one against all, dealing death against right, until that best of bright places stood black and bare.

And so it continued for a long spell: for twelve long winters Hrothgar was torn with distress, woes unceasing and side-piercing sorrows. The minstrels spread the sad news of Grendel's long drawn-out struggle with the dear Danish King, of plunder and outrage and savagery without ceasing; neither peace pact nor parley would he hold with any of the Danish host, nor desist from murder. Death was his only dealing.

Both young and old were pursued by the dark death-shadow of the monster. Through the long nights he marauded the misty moors. Men do not know where these hellish creatures range in their recklessness.

Thus the scourge of the warriors made many a fell swoop on their bodies in rapid succession. Heorot was his home—that black master of the once bright hall—each shadowy night.

Hrothgar, King of the Danes, was heartbroken by the wreck of his hopes for that high hall. Frequently they planned what was best to do to combat the reign of terror. Sometimes they vowed sacrifices at unholy places, and prayed to the devil himself to spare the people from the awful affliction. Such was the custom of the heathen who reverted to devilish practices in their ignorance. They lost sight of the Creator, the Judge of deeds; they lost sight of the worship of the King of Heaven, and His goodness.

Woe shall it be for those who are doomed to be destroyed in the everlasting fires of Hell, without help or hope!

Welcome shall it be for those who are destined to rest in the comfort of Heaven and God's warmth, for ever and ever!

gift-throne	The Anglo-Saxon (Old English) way of referring to a throne was often this combination '*gif-stol*'. It can be translated as 'gift-seat' or 'gift-throne' or simply 'throne'. Obviously from what the poet tells us time and time again in the story, the giving of gifts from the 'gift-throne' in the 'gift-hall' was one of the king's important duties.
Cain and Abel	You might like to look up the story of Cain and Abel. The story suggests that God's curse on Cain produced all kinds of evil things. Amongst them the story mentions *eotenas*, and *ylfe*, and *orcneas*, and *gigantas*. We could translate these as monsters (*eotenas*), elves (*ylfe*), evil spirits of the dead (*orcneas*), giants (*gigantas*). What do you think would be a good way of translating each of them?

Dictionary or discussion
  furbished
  fastness
  posse
  in a trice
  ravaged

Imagine you are a messenger sent to another country to get help for Hrothgar against Grendel. How would you relate Hrothgar's plight, and explain what was happening?

For discussion. Hrothgar's people feared the monster Grendel. Do we fear any monsters in the twentieth century?

Find out all about burial customs.

To do
Investigate the evidence we have of prehistoric monsters which actually existed. Were they as terrible as Grendel?
From the evidence in the story, describe a king's ship burial of long ago.
We do not know when the first story of Beowulf was composed. Do you think that at one time the story might have existed without mention of the Bible story, or God or hell? Would the story be poorer if they were not included in it?

Compose a poem on the death and ship burial of Scefing the Shield-King.

Improvise the death and burial of Scefing.

Make up a dance drama of Grendel the Monster.

Make up a story which ends with Scefing being found as a baby in a boat.

Project. Find out what religions existed in England between about A.D. 700 and 900.

United Press International

Give this picture a title.
Write a story, or poem, or song, or hymn, or an account of your thoughts and feelings as you look at it. Find and/or describe a suitable piece of music to go with this picture.

37

The School You Would Like?

The school I would like is one where there are young teachers, because I find that most teachers who have been teaching for a long time try to model schools on what it was like in their own schooldays when it was not as enjoyable as today.

MARK, 12

The teachers would be very young so that they would understand you more. There would be only one old person, that would be the cook. She would be very fat and jolly, with a loud laugh. The food that she cooks would be home-made and not dehydrated like some schools have.

JANIS, 14

I admit that if all the teachers were oldish men it would be a bit rough on the physical education teacher, although a small fat middle-aged man as a P.E. instructor would suit me perfectly.

KATHERINE, 12

I (2) **Of fools and knaves**

1. *'Here comes Doctor Brown,*
   The finest doctor in the town!'
2. *'But he hasn't got anything on!'*
3. *'I'll send for the Police!'*
4. *I may be a goon*
5. *Who can tell?*
6. *'Beowulf is my name!'*

'Here comes Doctor Brown,
The finest doctor in the town!'

Fools at the Fair

In the Middle Ages and for many years afterwards only a small proportion of the population of Europe inhabited cities and towns. The majority of the people lived and worked in villages or on farms. Most country people and many of the poorer people who lived in the towns never saw the jesters who amused the kings and queens. But, of course, the fools at the courts were not the only ones.

The fairs were very important events in those times. They were held in cities, in towns and sometimes in the villages. Some of the bigger fairs lasted for weeks. Traders came to a fair to sell their goods. Customers flocked to buy stocks of all those products they could not make or grow themselves: fine cloths, ornaments, spices and a hundred other things. Wandering doctors, who were called mountebanks, sold pills and ointments and boasted of the marvellous cures they could effect. Most of these mountebanks were accompanied by clowns whose antics attracted patients. Sellers of sweetmeats did a roaring trade. All was bustle and excitement, especially for those who could only visit a fair perhaps once a year. The crowds enjoyed it all. But, more than anything else, they were delighted by the entertainers who were always present. . . .

There were story-tellers, musicians and ballad singers. These were often dressed in short blue coats, yellow belts and red stockings. There were no circuses, but there were performing animals: monkeys which could somersault, dancing bears, dogs and horses which could do clever tricks, and sometimes even hares which had been trained to beat drums with their paws. There were strong men and wrestlers; tumblers, conjurers and jugglers; and, of course, at every fair there were the funny fools.

Sometimes these clowns were not simply called jesters or fools. Merry Andrew, Zany and Jack Pudding were some of their names. Often one of the clowns pretended to be a jester who had performed before royalty. He was dressed in cap and bells and motley. Others wore costumes which were all patches. . . .

They made them, as clowns have always done, as funny and as ridiculous as possible.

The entertainers wandered from fair to fair. The more adventurous of these wanderers, including some who were clowns, went from country to country just as many circus people do today. In Germany, one type of clown was always called English John—even if he were a German, a Frenchman or of any other nationality.

When fairs were not being held, the wanderers roamed the country in little bands, giving their acts in market-places, villages and even in isolated farmhouses. The country people collected to see the turns and to watch, listen to and laugh at the clowns.

There were so many of these wandering entertainers during the reign of Queen Elizabeth I that they were classed with 'rogues, vagabonds and sturdy beggars'. As a result they were liable to be whipped and put into the stocks. But that did not stop them giving their shows. After they were punished they moved on to districts where they were welcome.

Sometimes the wanderers, and especially the clowns among them, got into trouble for other reasons. One such clown was William Philips, who gave an act at St Bartholomew's Fair. He made some very witty jokes against the government of the day. Usually jesters were allowed to say what they liked but on this occasion Philips was arrested, whipped publicly and warned to be careful what he said.

'I'll hold my tongue in future,' he promised the authorities.

Naturally people were eager to know what he would do during his next performance. So were the authorities.

He appeared with a grin on his face, made jokes about his whipping, and then held up his hand. In it was a tongue he had bought from a butcher's stall.

'I'm doing what I promised,' he said, to the laughter of the crowds. 'I'm holding my tongue!'

All these wandering performers made their living from giving shows. But there were others.

At Christmas, and sometimes during other holidays, groups of English villagers dressed themselves up and performed sword and morris dances. There was always a clown in each group; sometimes he was a man dressed up in women's clothes and called a Bessy.

Other villagers gave little plays. The amateur actors who performed them were called mummers. They wore masks or blackened their faces with soot. Some dressed up in the skins and tails of animals. Others decked themselves out in twigs. Still more wore any odd mixture of clothes that would raise laughs.

The plays they performed had been handed down for generations – and had got all mixed up in the process. But the mummers did not worry about that, nor did the people who watched them. The plays gave a fine excuse for clowning.

Many of the plays had begun as religious stories and a great favourite was *St George and the Dragon*. But by the time the mummers had altered it, all that remained of the original story was the fight!

A player who was called the Fool, Merry Andrew or any other name meaning clown, would speak in rhymes, telling the audience of the play it was going to see. Then two of the characters would put on a mock fight with wooden swords. One man would fall down, give terrible groans and pretend to be killed. The first player would then call out:

> Here comes Doctor Brown,
> The finest doctor in the town!

In would walk a mummer dressed as a doctor. He would boast:

> I can make dead men alive!

'Doctor' Brown and another mummer who was usually called Jack Finney would clown around the fallen man. The 'Doctor' would give Jack Finney ridiculous orders and Jack Finney would suggest impossible ways of curing the fallen man. Everyone would get in everyone else's way, then the fallen man would spring up, declare he was cured and begin to fight again. And so it would go on until it was time to move to the next house and repeat the performance.

Only the person who introduced the actors was called by a name meaning clown, but every one of the party of mummers clowned and jested through the performance.

JOHN HORNBY: *Clowns through the Ages*

Questions
What might you have found at a fair in the Middle Ages?
What kind of life did an entertainer lead in the Middle Ages?
How did Philips make a fool of the authorities?

Discussion
What makes people laugh?
What makes *you* laugh? (At home? In films? On television? In books?)
Which do you enjoy more – funny things or serious things?

Writing
Describe a fair in the Middle Ages as you imagine it might have been. (Where can you find out more about it? What *were* the 'Middle Ages'?)
Describe your idea of a perfect April Fool's Day prank.

Improvisation
Invent a performance by one of the fools at the fair. (You might be a strong man, wrestler, tumbler, conjurer, juggler, animal trainer, or any other character who takes part in the performance.)
Perform the play of St George and the Dragon.
Find and act one of the Robin Hood plays.
Improvise a medieval market scene. Include stall-holders, beggars, customers, bystanders, pickpockets and thieves. (What is the origin of the word *cutpurse*?)

Records
Till Eulenspiegel, by Richard Strauss, is a piece of music about the joker, Till Eulenspiegel.
The Dance of the Buffoons, from Rimsky-Korsakov's opera *The Snow Maiden*.
You should be able to find both of these in a record catalogue.

Reading
Clowns through the Ages by John Hornby (Oliver and Boyd).

Picture
How much can you see in this picture?
What does the picture suggest to you?
Try to describe the picture to someone who doesn't have a copy of it.
Write a story based on the picture, or make up and act a play about the characters in the picture.
Close the book. How many of the details in the picture can you write down from memory in ten minutes?

'But he hasn't got anything on!'

The Emperor's New Clothes

Many years ago there lived an Emperor who was so monstrous
fond of fine new clothes that he spent all his money on being
really smart. He didn't care about his army, he didn't care for
going to the play, or driving out in the park, unless it was to show
his new clothes. He had a coat for every hour in the day; and
just as people say about a king that 'he's holding a council', so
in this country they always said, 'The Emperor is in his dressing-
room.' In the great city where he lived, life was very pleasant,
lots of strangers came there every day; and one day there arrived
two swindlers. They gave out that they were weavers, and said
they knew how to make the loveliest stuff that could possibly be
imagined. Not only were the colours and patterns extraordinarily
pretty, but the clothes that were made of the stuff had this
marvellous property: that they were invisible to anyone who
was either unfit for his situation or else was intolerably stupid.
'Very excellent clothes those must be,' thought the Emperor.
'If I wore them I could tell which are the men in my realm who
are't fit for the posts they hold. I could tell clever people from
stupid ones: to be sure that stuff must be made for me directly.'
Accordingly he gave the two swindlers a large sum in advance
so that they might begin their work. They set up two looms and
pretended to be working, but they hadn't a vestige of anything
on the looms. In hot haste they demanded the finest of silk and
the best of gold, which they stuffed into their own pockets; and
they worked away at the bare looms till any hour of the night.
   'I *should* like to know how they are getting on,' thought the
Emperor. . . . ,
   At last he decided to see. . . .
   'Will Your Imperial Majesty be graciously pleased to take off
your clothes?' said the swindlers. 'We can then put the new ones
upon you here, before the large mirror.' The Emperor took off all
his clothes, and the swindlers behaved as if they were handing
him each piece of the new suit which was supposed to have been
made; and they put their hands about his waist and pretended

to tie something securely. It was the train. The Emperor turned and twisted himself in front of the glass.

'Heaven! How well it fits! How beautifully it sits,' said everyone. 'The pattern! The colours! It is indeed a noble costume!'

'They are waiting, outside, with the canopy which is to be borne over Your Majesty in the procession,' said the chief master of the ceremonies. 'Very well, I am ready,' said the Emperor. 'Doesn't it sit well?' Once more he turned about in front of the glass that it might seem as if he was really examining his finery. The lords in waiting, who were to carry the train, fumbled with their hands in the direction of the floor as if they were picking the train up. They walked on, holding the air – they didn't want to let it be noticed that they could see nothing at all.

So the Emperor walked in the procession under the beautiful canopy, and everybody in the streets and at the windows said: 'Lord! How splendid the Emperor's new clothes are! What a lovely train he has to his coat! What a beautiful fit it is!' Nobody wanted to be detected seeing nothing: that would mean that he was no good at his job, or that he was very stupid. None of the Emperor's costumes had ever been such a success.

'But he hasn't got anything on!' said a little child. 'Lor! Just hark at the innocent,' said its father. And one whispered to the other what the child had said: 'That little child there says he hasn't got anything on.'

'Why, he hasn't got anything on!' the whole crowd was shouting at last; and the Emperor's flesh crept, for it seemed to him they were right. 'But all the same,' he thought to himself, 'I must go through with the procession.' So he held himself more proudly than before, and the lords in waiting walked on bearing the train – the train that wasn't there at all.

HANS ANDERSEN: *Forty-two Stories*
(*translated by M. R. James*)

Questions
What did the Emperor care about most?
What story did the two swindlers tell?
Why did the Emperor give the swindlers money?
Why were the swindlers able to deceive everyone?
Who eventually gave the game away?

Writing
Imagine you were in the crowd watching the Emperor's procession. Write a report for a newspaper describing the procession and the reactions of the onlookers.

Discussion
New clothes.

Project
Find out how dress and fashion have changed through the ages, and what variations exist in the world today. How has progress in the discovery of new materials affected fashion?
Find out more about Hans Andersen, his life and stories.

Film
Hans Christian Andersen (Danny Kaye), 1952.

Dictionary
    gave out (in sense of 'led people to believe')
    vestige

'I'll send for the Police!'

Some Hallucinations

> He thought he saw an Elephant,
>   That practised on a fife:
> He looked again, and found it was
>   A letter from his wife.
> 'At length I realize,' he said,
>   'The bitterness of Life!'
>
> He thought he saw a Buffalo
>   Upon the chimney-piece:
> He looked again, and found it was
>   His Sister's Husband's Niece.
> 'Unless you leave this house,' he said,
>   'I'll send for the Police!'
>
> He thought he saw a Rattlesnake
>   That questioned him in Greek:
> He looked again, and found it was
>   The Middle of Next Week.
> 'The one thing I regret,' he said,
>   'Is that it cannot speak!'
>
> He thought he saw a Banker's Clerk
>   Descending from the bus:
> He looked again, and found it was
>   A Hippopotamus:
> 'If this should stay to dine,' he said,
>   'There won't be much for us!'

LEWIS CARROLL

Invent some more 'hallucinations'.

'I may be a goon'

Musician's Lament

I may be a goon
On the bassoon
But I can blow.
I may be dumb
On the drum
Or piccolo.
I'm inclined to dither
On the zither
Or the flute.
When I sing
People fling
Fruit.

DAVID MOWBRAY (aged twelve)

Write some more laments.

50

Make up a script to go with these pictures.
Give each of the pictures a caption.

'Who can tell?'

The Lobster Pot

> Who can tell how the lobster got
> Into the lobster pot?
> When he went in he did not doubt
> There was a passage out.
> There was not.

JOHN ARDEN

Write a story or poem about a lobster setting a trap and catching a man in it.

Picture

Give this picture a title.

Describe this picture accurately and in detail.

Write a story called 'The most interesting character I have ever met' *or* tell a story as if you were someone or something in the picture – you might, for example, speak as if you were the rabbit, or the window, or the doorway, or the brush, or the person in the doorway. You could, if you wished, make them all speak to one another, as though they were characters in a play, or dream, or nightmare, or fantasy.

Write a story or play which ends: 'So it all goes to show, it's not where you have been but where you are going that matters.'

53

'Beowulf is my name!'

Beowulf—2

The minstrel tells how Beowulf hears of Hrothgar's troubles, and sets sail from Southern Sweden to help him:

Hrothgar brooded helplessly over the deep distress of his fortunes. The wise warrior could not combat the horror; the terror by night was too much for him, too overwhelming, too savage. But over the seas in Sweden the news reached a good prince called Beowulf. He was the strongest of men in those troubled times, mighty by birth and bearing.

He ordered a good ship to be got ready. He said he would seek out Hrothgar over the swan's road, since the brave soldier stood in need of men. Though Beowulf was well beloved, his wise people did not blame him for setting out on such a task. Rather, they encouraged him. He selected fourteen of the bravest warriors he could find amongst his own countrymen, and, skilled seaman that he was, himself led them to the shore.

Soon their boat was launched, riding the waves in sight of the steep cliffs. Fully armed, the warriors embarked by the prow; the waves churned the sand; men loaded the bottom of the ship with bright weapons and shields; the warriors on their eager expedition pushed off their well-built boat. Then just like a bird, urged on by the wind, it flew over the surge, with foam at its neck, until the time came on the second day when the proud ship had sight of land, shimmering sea cliffs, high fells and jutting promontories. The sea voyage was over, the passage completed.

Then without delay Beowulf's warriors disembarked, and moored their sea vessel securely, their weapons and armour ringing out bravely. They gave thanks to God for their safe-keeping over the sea-paths.

Then from the fortifications the Danish coastguard whose duty it was to watch the shores for invaders saw the warriors carrying their bright shields and weapons of war over the gang-plank. He was much troubled about the identity of these strangers. Hrothgar's guard galloped down to the shore, bravely brandishing his great spear, and challenged the newcomers thus:

'Are you friend or foe who land here over the ocean way, bristling with armour and the appearance of aggression, with your towering ship? For many a day I have kept watch on this coast, so that no storm troops might take us by surprise, stealing over the sea on to Danish soil. No foreigners have ever landed here more brashly with their war weapons; nor have you sought permission to land from our people. Never have I seen a mightier prince on earth, clad for the fray, than the one I spot in your midst. He is no simple soldier bedecked with weapons, unless appearance and bearing deceive me.

'Now I must know where you come from before you go a step further on Danish soil. For all I know, you might be foreign spies. Now, you adventurers from afar, carried hither by the sea, bend your ears to my speech. It would be better for you to state at once why and whence you come!'

The minstrel relates how Beowulf sets the coastguard's mind at rest:

Beowulf the leader of the party, unlocked the secret of their errand: 'We are from Sweden, and serve Hygelac the King. My father was well known among all men for his prowess in battle. He lived to a brave old age, and at his death there were none who knew him not. We have come to present ourselves to Hrothgar, your King, in peace and friendship; guide us well! We have a great task to accomplish for your King, and no one shall remain in ignorance for long about our mission.

'You will be only too well aware, if rumour runs aright, that amongst the Danes dwells some kind of terror, a hateful monstrosity, who in the depths of night perpetrates horrors unspeakable and shameful indignities. I come with open-handed advice to Hrothgar, to show how he might end his troubles, if fate ordains that there might ever be an end to his sore afflictions, the devastations, the suffering. Do you wish these crushing torments to continue as long as that fine feasting hall stands stoutly there?'

The coastguard answered from the safety of his horse: 'A soldier who is worth his salt must distinguish between words and deeds! I accept that this is a troop friendly to the King of the Danes. You may pass, bearing your weapons and armour; I will show you the way. Moreover, I will give orders for my men to protect your sea-craft from pirates. Your newly-tarred transport, with the ornate prow, will be safe on the sands, until the time comes for it to carry you again over the swirling seas to the shores of your homeland. To such a man as you, fate will grant safe conduct through the rush of battle.'

Thus they set off on their way. Their ship bobbed safely at anchor, its broad beam riding the swell. Above the warriors' helmets shone boar crests of burnished gold, fire-hardened and fierce to protect them. They made a route march all together until that high timbered hall towered in view, stately and strutted with gold. Hrothgar's seat was the most celebrated in the world, and its legend spread far to many lands. The coast-guard confirmed that this was their destination, and urged them thither. Facing his horse about, he said: 'It is time for me to leave you. May the Almighty Father protect you by His grace, and see you safely through your task. I must return to the sea to guard against unwelcome invaders.'

The minstrel tells how Beowulf's party are again challenged, this time by Wulfgar, King Hrothgar's herald:

The way was paved with stone which guided the men along together. Their coats of mail, iron-hard and hand-linked, shone and jangled at their approach. When they entered the Hall, weary with their long travel, they rested their toughened shields against the palace wall; they sat down on the bench; their coats of mail, soldier's attire, rang out. Their grey-tipped ash spears stood arrayed neatly together. They were not short of weapons.

There, at the entrance, a proud Dane again interrogated them and demanded their credentials: 'From whence have you brought these ornate shields, grey corselets and grim helmets? I am a representative and officer of Hrothgar. Never before have I seen a foreign band so rashly bold, though I trust you come of your own free will as itinerant adventurers rather than exiled outcasts to Hrothgar's doors!'

Boldly Beowulf replied to this challenge, handsome and hardy under his boar helmet: 'We are subjects of Hygelac. Beowulf is my name. I shall announce my business to your King Hrothgar himself, if he will be so gracious as to welcome us.'

Wulfgar, a wise warrior, replied: 'I will acquaint Hrothgar, the ring giver and renowned prince of Heorot, with your words, and shortly will return with his reply.'

Then he returned swiftly to where Hrothgar sat, old and grey among his band of nobles. As was the custom, Wulfgar approached till he stood face to face with his King, and addressed him in this fashion: 'Far from over the sea have arrived a force of warriors. Beowulf is the name of their leader. They wish to make themselves and their errand known to you personally. Listen to what they have to say, gracious Hrothgar! Their carriage and equipment betoken nobility. Their chief who has led them here is no mean hero!'

Imagine that you are one of the men who accompanied Beowulf on his expedition, and you have the opportunity to send a letter home to say what kind of a journey and reception you have had. Write the letter, describing the voyage, the challenges and the replies.

For discussion. Are appearances deceptive?

Find out all about the ships of the sixth century and thereabouts.

Writing
Make up the reply that you imagine Hrothgar might make to Wulfgar.
Was it more exciting to live in the days of Beowulf?
Write a poem about the journey of Beowulf and his men over the sea.

Improvisation
See if you can give an impression of the ship in which Beowulf sailed. Make a short play out of the meetings between Beowulf and the coastguard and Beowulf and Wulfgar. Either write your own dialogue, or use the words from the extract. How would you describe the coastguard? How would you describe Wulfgar? How would you describe Beowulf? When you are acting these parts, try to make use of your descriptions in your performance.

I (3) Of fighting of many kinds

1. 'I had the best black eye in Wales, perhaps it was the best black eye in Europe!'
2. Clammy fingers were feeling for his throat.
3. 'You should have thought of all this before you were born.'
4. The summer of fear.
5. What a dandy fellow!
6. 'I shall come to grips with the ghoul!'

When we look at our schools today and politicians say we've got one of the best educational systems in the world, we realize how low standards must be.

Why do we go to school? Do we go to learn what two and two add up to? Do we go to learn how to play netball? Is not the idea of going to school to learn to 'get on' with other people, to learn to share and help, to learn to enjoy and to be stimulated and satisfied? Surely getting a detention for speaking is not helping towards these things? In the school I would like, the relationship between teacher and pupil would be changed. Instead of the teacher *telling* the pupil, both teacher and pupil would learn together, creating warm relationships, clear understanding and a zest for knowledge. We *know* that anyone, if treated as a human being and not bawled at for dropping a ruler, etc., can get on and will.

For good academic standards to exist there must be a will to learn. In the majority of schools today there is no will to learn, and that is why many children wish to leave school early. . . .

The pupils would have great freedom, restrictions would be minimized. If a pupil wished to stay on to work or play, that pupil would be permitted to. The school need not be lavish, though pleasant surroundings would help everyone to be happier. With a small amount of money and a large amount of care, the school could be a place which was loved by everyone.

In this type of school, free expression, free thought, freedom to work at one's own pace would exist. In this school, hours would pass pleasantly, 'lessons' would not exist because the pupils would have time to find out why, when and how.

The pupils would talk freely about religion, politics, music, sport or whatever else they would wish to discuss. They would quietly (or loudly) debate, read and laugh. It would be a place where the pupils would be learning to live with each other and with 'outsiders', i.e. teachers; also a place for reasoning, cogitating, studying about things of importance to mankind.

Who knows – perhaps among the pupils of Britain one would turn out to be an inventor of a method for feeding the starving. . . .

This is a school! A place where people together learn to live together and love one another, where people learn to reason, learn to understand and above all learn to think for themselves. School was not invented just for the little people to become the same as the big people, but for the pupils to learn how to live and let live. Money is not what is needed so much as common sense, and the school I would like – in fact, the school I long for – would be a thing of the present. Now!

JUDITH, 13

'*I had the best black eye in Wales!*'

The Fight

I was standing at the end of the lower playground annoying Mr Samuels, who lived in the house just below the high railings. Mr Samuels complained once a week that boys from the school threw apples and stones and balls through his bedroom window. He sat in a deck chair in a small square of trim garden and tried to read the newspaper. I was only a few yards from him. I was staring him out. He pretended not to notice me, but I knew he knew I was standing there rudely and quietly. Every now and then he peeped at me from behind his newspaper, saw me still and serious and alone, with my eyes on his. As soon as he lost his temper I was going to go home. Already I was late for dinner. I had almost beaten him, the newspaper was trembling, he was breathing heavily, when a strange boy, whom I had not heard approach, pushed me down the bank.

I threw a stone at his face. He took off his spectacles, put them in his coat pocket, took off his coat, hung it neatly on the railings, and attacked. Turning round as we wrestled on the top of the bank, I saw that Mr Samuels had folded his newspaper on the deck chair and was standing up to watch us. It was a mistake to turn round. The strange boy rabbit-punched me twice. Mr Samuels hopped with excitement as I fell against the railings. I was down in the dust, hot and scratched and biting, then up and dancing, and I butted the boy in the belly and we tumbled in a heap. I saw through a closing eye that his nose was bleeding. I hit his nose. He tore at my collar and spun me round by the hair.

'Come on! come on!' I heard Mr Samuels cry.

We both turned towards him. He was shaking his fists and dodging about in the garden. He stopped then, and coughed, and set his panama straight, and avoided our eyes, and turned his back and walked slowly to the deck chair.

We both threw gravel at him.

'I'll give him "Come on!" ' the boy said, as we ran along the playground away from the shouts of Mr Samuels and down the steps on to the hill.

We walked home together. I admired his bloody nose. He said that my eye was like a poached egg, only black.

'I've never seen such a lot of blood,' I said.

He said I had the best black eye in Wales, perhaps it was the best black eye in Europe!

'And there's blood all over your shirt.'

'Sometimes I bleed in dollops,' he said.

On Walter's Road we passed a group of high school girls, and I cocked my cap and hoped my eye was as big as a bluebag, and he walked with his coat flung open to show the bloodstains.

I was a hooligan all during dinner, and a bully, and as bad as a boy from the Sandbanks, and I should have more respect, and I sat silently over the sago pudding. That afternoon I went to school with an eye-shade on. If I had had a black silk sling I would have been as gay and desperate as the wounded captain in the book that my sister used to read, and that I read under the bedclothes at night, secretly with a flash-lamp.

On the road, a boy from an inferior school, where the parents did not have to pay anything, called me 'One eye!' in a harsh, adult voice. I took no notice, but walked along whistling, my good eye on the summer clouds sailing, beyond insult, above Terrace Road.

The mathematics master said: 'I see that Mr Thomas at the back of the class has been straining his eyesight. But it isn't over his homework, is it, gentlemen?'

Gilbert Rees, next to me, laughed loudest.

'I'll break your leg after school!' I said.

He'd hobble, howling, up to the headmaster's study. A deep hush in the school. A message on a plate brought by the porter.

'The headmaster's compliments, sir, and will you come at once?'

'How did you happen to break this boy's leg?' 'Oh! damn and bottom, the agony!' cried Gilbert Rees. 'Just a little twist,' I would say. 'I don't know my own strength. I apologize. But there's nothing to worry about. Let me set the leg, sir.' A rapid manipulation, the click of a bone. 'Doctor Thomas, sir, at your service.' Mrs Rees was on her knees. 'How can I thank you?' 'It's nothing at all, dear lady. Wash his ears every morning. Throw away his rulers. Pour his red and green inks down the sink.'

In Mr Trotter's drawing class we drew naked girls inaccurately on sheets of paper under our drawings of a vase and passed them along under the desks. Some of the drawings were detailed strangely, others were tailed off like mermaids. Gilbert Rees drew the vase only.

'What would you do if you had a million pounds?'

'I'd buy a Bugatti and a Rolls and a Bentley and I'd go two hundred miles an hour on Pendine sands.'

'I'd buy a harem and keep the girls in the gym.'

'I'd buy a house like Mrs Cotmore-Richards', twice as big as hers, and a cricket field and a football field and a proper garage with mechanics and a lift.'

'And a lavatory as big as, as big as the Melba pavilion, with plush seats and a golden chain and. . . .'

'And I'd smoke cigarettes with real gold tips, better than Morris's Blue Book.'

'I'd buy all the railway trains, and only 4A could travel in them.'

'And not Gilbert Rees either.'

'What's the longest you've been?'

'I went to Edinburgh.'

'My father went to Salonika in the War.'

'Where's that, Cyril?'

'Cave!'[1]

'Hide your drawings.'

'I bet you a greyhound can go faster than a horse.'

Everybody liked the drawing class, except Mr Trotter.

DYLAN THOMAS

Questions
Do you feel sorry for Mr Samuels?
How would you describe the mathematics master's tone of voice?
Why does he speak like this, do you think?
Does the narrator break Gilbert's leg?

Discussion
'Free expression.'

Writing
Write on one of the following themes: a friendship with a strange beginning; a boaster; a liar; an incident with a neighbour; a fight; a meeting in the road; a 'toady'.

[1] 'Look out!'

In this extract the narrator makes up a fantasy in which everything turns out unexpectedly well for him. Write a fantasy of your own.

What would *you* do if you had a million pounds?

Write character sketches of the narrator, Dan, Gilbert Rees and Mr Trotter.

Tape

Make a tape recording of sounds and events to give a picture of an imaginary school.

Improvisation

Discover ways of acting the incidents or fantasies in this extract, without actually hurting your opponent. (How are fights staged on television? Do the actors really get hurt?)

Records

If you enjoyed this piece of writing by Dylan Thomas you might like to listen to some of these records:

Dylan Thomas reading Quite Early One Morning and other memories (Caedmon Literary Series TC 1132)

Under Milk Wood (Caedmon Literary Series TC 0996 0997).

'Clammy fingers were feeling for his throat!'

In 'English 11/12' you met 'The Hobbit'. You will remember that hobbits are 'a little people, smaller than the bearded Dwarves . . . are inclined to be fat in the stomach . . . wear no shoes, because their feet grow natural leathery soles and thick warm brown hair like the stuff on their heads'. Of Gollum, the author says: 'I don't know where he came from, nor who or what he was. He was Gollum – as dark as darkness . . . when he said 'gollum' he made a horrible swallowing noise in his throat. That is how he got his name, though he always called himself "my precious".'

In 'The Lord of the Rings', another much longer tale which involves the hobbits and Gollum, the story tells how two hobbits, Sam and Frodo, spot Gollum crawling towards them.

The moon now rode high and clear. Its thin white light lit up the faces of the rocks and drenched the cold frowning walls of the cliff, turning all the wide looming darkness into a chill pale grey scored with black shadows.

'Well!' said Frodo, standing up and drawing his cloak more closely round him. 'You sleep for a bit, Sam, and take my blanket. I'll walk up and down on sentry for a while.' Suddenly he stiffened, and stooping he gripped Sam by the arm. 'What's that?' he whispered. 'Look over there on the cliff!'

Sam looked and breathed in sharply through his teeth.

'Ssss!' he said. 'That's what it is. It's that Gollum! Snakes and adders! And to think that I thought that we'd puzzle him with our bit of a climb! Look at him! Like a nasty crawling spider on a wall.'

Down the face of a precipice, sheer and almost smooth it seemed in the pale moonlight, a small black shape was moving with its thin limbs splayed out. Maybe its soft clinging hands and toes were finding crevices and holds that no hobbit could ever have seen or used, but it looked as if it was just creeping down on sticky pads, like some large prowling thing of insect-kind. And it was coming down head first, as if it was smelling its way. Now and again it lifted its head slowly, turning it right back on its long skinny neck, and the hobbits caught a glimpse of two small pale gleaming lights, its eyes that blinked at the moon for a moment and then were quickly lidded again.

'Do you think he can see us?' said Sam.

'I don't know,' said Frodo quietly, 'but I think not. It is hard even for friendly eyes to see these elven-cloaks: I cannot see you in the shadow even at a few paces. And I've heard that he doesn't like Sun or Moon.'

'Then why is he coming down just here?' asked Sam.

'Quietly, Sam!' said Frodo. 'He can smell us, perhaps. And he can hear as keen as Elves, I believe. I think he has heard something now: our voices probably. We did a lot of shouting away back there; and we were talking far too loudly until a minute ago.'

'Well, I'm sick of him,' said Sam. 'He's come once too often for me, and I'm going to have a word with him, if I can. I don't suppose we could give him the slip now anyway.' Drawing his grey hood well over his face, Sam crept stealthily towards the cliff.

'Careful!' whispered Frodo coming behind. 'Don't alarm him! He's much more dangerous than he looks.'

The black crawling shape was now three-quarters of the way down, and perhaps fifty feet or less above the cliff's foot. Crouching stone-still in the shadow of a large boulder the hobbits watched him. He seemed to have come to a difficult passage or to be troubled about something. They could hear him snuffling, and now and again there was a harsh hiss of breath that sounded like a curse. He lifted his head, and they thought they heard him spit. Then he moved on again. Now they could hear his voice creaking and whistling.

'Ach, sss! Cautious, my precious! More haste less speed. We musstn't rissk our neck, musst we, precious? No, precious – *gollum!*' He lifted his head again, blinked at the moon, and quickly shut his eyes. 'We hate it,' he hissed. 'Nassty, nassty shivery light it is -sss- it spies on us, precious – it hurts our eyes.'

He was getting lower now and the hisses became sharper and clearer.

'Where iss it, where iss it: my precious, my precious? It's ours, it is, and we want it. The thieves, the thieves, the filthy little thieves. Where are they with my precious? Curse them! We hates them.'

'It doesn't sound as if he knew we were here, does it?' whispered Sam. 'And what's his precious? Does he mean the –'

'Hsh!' breathed Frodo. 'He's getting near now, near enough to hear a whisper.'

Indeed Gollum had suddenly paused again, and his large head on its scrawny neck was lolling from side to side as if he was listening. His pale eyes were half unlidded. Sam restrained himself, though his fingers were twitching. His eyes, filled with anger and disgust, were fixed on the wretched creature as he now began to move again, still whispering and hissing to himself.

At last he was no more than a dozen feet from the ground, right above their heads. From that point there was a sheer drop, for the cliff was slightly undercut, and even Gollum could not find a hold of any kind. He seemed to be trying to twist round, so as to go legs first, when suddenly with a shrill whistling shriek he fell. As he did so, he curled his legs and arms up round him, like a spider whose descending thread is snapped.

Sam was out of his hiding in a flash and crossed the space between him and the cliff-foot in a couple of leaps. Before Gollum could get up, he was on top of him. But he found Gollum more than he bargained for, even taken like that, suddenly, off his guard after a fall. Before Sam could get a hold, long legs and arms were wound round him pinning his arms, and a clinging grip, soft but horribly strong, was squeezing him like slowly tightening cords; clammy fingers were feeling for his throat. Then sharp teeth bit into his shoulder. All he could do was to butt his hard round head sideways into the creature's face. Gollum hissed and spat, but he did not let go.

Things would have gone ill with Sam, if he had been alone. But Frodo sprang up, and drew Sting from its sheath. With his left hand he drew back Gollum's head by its thin lank hair, stretching its long neck, and forcing his pale venomous eyes to stare up at the sky.

'Let go! Gollum,' he said. 'This is Sting. You have seen it before once upon a time. Let go, or you'll feel it this time! I'll cut your throat.'

Gollum collapsed and went as loose as wet string. Sam got up, fingering his shoulder. His eyes smouldered with anger, but he could not avenge himself: his miserable enemy lay grovelling on the stones whimpering.

'Don't hurt us! Don't let them hurt us, precious! They won't hurt us will they, nice little hobbitses? We didn't mean no harm, but they jumps on us like cats on poor mices, they did, precious.

And we're so lonely, *gollum*. We'll be nice to them, very nice, if they'll be nice to us, won't we, yes, yess.'

'Well, what's to be done with it?' said Sam. 'Tie it up, so as it can't come sneaking after us no more, I say.'

'But that would kill us, kill us,' whimpered Gollum. 'Cruel little hobbitses. Tie us up in the cold hard lands and leave us, *gollum, gollum*.' Sobs welled up in his gobbling throat.

'No,' said Frodo. 'If we kill him, we must kill him outright. But we can't do that, not as things are. Poor wretch! He has done us no harm.'

'Oh hasn't he!' said Sam rubbing his shoulder. 'Anyway he meant to, and he means to, I'll warrant. Throttle us in our sleep, that's his plan.'

'I daresay,' said Frodo. 'But what he means to do is another matter.' He paused for a while in thought. Gollum lay still, but stopped whimpering. Sam stood glowering over him.

It seemed to Frodo then that he heard, quite plainly but far off, voices out of the past:

> *What a pity Bilbo did not stab the vile creature, when he had a chance! Pity? It was Pity that stayed his hand. Pity, and Mercy: not to strike without need.*
>
> *I do not feel any pity for Gollum. He deserves death. And some die that deserve life. Can you give that to them? Then be not eager to deal out death in the name of justice, fearing for your own safety. Even the wise cannot see all ends.*

J. R. R. TOLKIEN: The Two Towers

Questions
What has Gollum in common with human beings?
What makes him different from human beings?
Is there anything in the passage which makes you suspect that Gollum is not to be trusted?

What have the hobbits in common with human beings?
What makes them different from human beings?

What is 'Sting'?

'Even the wise cannot see all ends.' What does this mean?

Discussion
Should Bilbo have stabbed Gollum when he had the chance? (When do you think people should have pity or mercy? Do you

dislike Gollum, or are you sorry for him? Do you think the author has made Gollum too bad? Not bad enough? What do you think of the hobbits' reactions to him?)

Improvisation
Work out an episode showing why Gollum calls the hobbits 'thieves'.

Writing
Invent a character from the land of 'fairy', and write an adventure involving the character you invent.

Reading
The Lord of the Rings:
   Part 1 'The Fellowship of the Ring'
   Part 2 'The Two Towers'
   Part 3 'The Return of the King'.

(*The Lord of the Rings* is by J. R. R. Tolkien. It is published by Allen and Unwin and is available in paperback.)

The School You Would Like?
The pupils should be given more chance to speak and the teacher should be given a chance to listen.

SUSAN, 13

'You should have thought of all this before you were born.'

A living room in a suburban home. The father is busy with his work. The mother moves to and from the kitchen doing her work. The daughter stands on a chair to look at herself in the wall mirror, holding her hands straight to her sides.

MRS GROOMKIRBY: I thought you'd gone, Sylvia.

SYLVIA: How can I go out with my arms like this? Look at them!

MRS GROOMKIRBY: What's the matter with your arms?

SYLVIA: You can see what's the matter with them. You've only got to look at them.

MRS GROOMKIRBY: You've been out with them like that often enough before. I can't see anything wrong with them.

SYLVIA: They're absolutely ridiculous!

MRS GROOMKIRBY: Turn round and let me see. Hold them naturally! They look just the same to me as they always do.

SYLVIA: That doesn't make them any better. Look where they reach to!

MRS GROOMKIRBY: I'm looking, Sylvia. They're perfectly all right. It's the proper length for them. Mine are exactly the same. So are your father's.

MR GROOMKIRBY: Hm?

SYLVIA: Oh for goodness' sake, mum!

(*Pause*)

MRS GROOMKIRBY: (*off*) What time's Stan supposed to be coming?

SYLVIA: (*fuming*) Quarter of an hour ago!

(*Pause*)

If they started lower down it would be something.

MRS GROOMKIRBY: What difference would that make?

(*Pause*)

SYLVIA: Look where they reach to! Just look at that gap.

MRS GROOMKIRBY: What gap?

SYLVIA: There!

MRS GROOMKIRBY: I don't know what you're talking about, Sylvia. I can't see any gap.

(*Pause*)

72

SYLVIA: If they didn't *start* so blessed high up I might be able to reach my knees with them!

(*Pause*)

MRS GROOMKIRBY: (*off*) It's beyond me, Sylvia, why you should want to reach your knees with them!

(*off*) In any case you can bend down and do it, can't you?

SYLVIA: I don't *want* to have to bend down! That's the whole point!

(*Pause*)

MRS GROOMKIRBY: (*off*) I suppose it's Stan we've got to thank for this.

SYLVIA: Oh – Stan, Stan, Stan! I wish you wouldn't keep on about *Stan* all the time! It's nothing to do with Stan.

(*Pause*)

MRS GROOMKIRBY: (*off*) In any case there isn't anything we can do about it now. You should have thought of all this before you were born.

SYLVIA: For goodness' sake, mum! How *could* I have?

MRS GROOMKIRBY: We're not turning you into some monstrosity or other just to satisfy one of your whims, Sylvia.

SYLVIA: (*scornfully*) Whim!

MRS GROOMKIRBY: Making you look like an ape.

(*Pause*)

SYLVIA: At least apes can reach their knees without bending.

MRS GROOMKIRBY: Apes are bending all the time, Sylvia. As you well know.

(*Pause*)

SYLVIA: Not all that much.

(*Pause*)

MR GROOMKIRBY: You'd need a complete new set of glands, Sylvia. We couldn't run to it.

MRS GROOMKIRBY: (*off*) She's spending too much time at the Zoo.

(*Pause*)

SYLVIA: I don't know what it is you've got against apes as far as that goes.

MRS GROOMKIRBY: (*off*) We've got nothing against apes, Sylvia. As such.

(*Long pause*)

I thought we were leading up to something like this when you started on about your arms in the first place.

SYLVIA: Oh!

MRS GROOMKIRBY: (*off*) It's only since you've been going to the Zoo with Stan two or three times a week that we've had all this.

SYLVIA: For the last time will you shut up about Stan, mum? For God's sake! It's got nothing to do with Stan! Or the Zoo either as far as that goes.

MRS GROOMKIRBY: (*off*) What with that and the Natural History Museum every weekend, I'm not surprised she gets hold of all these idiotic ideas.

(*Pause*)

Spending all her time amongst a lot of mastodons and pterodactyls.

(*Pause*)

I blame Stan for all this, you know.

MR GROOMKIRBY: Hm?

N. F. SIMPSON

Questions

What prevents Sylvia from going out?

How does Mrs Groomkirby try to deal with Sylvia?

(What different tactics does she employ? What does she say to show that she does not think there is anything wrong with Sylvia's arms? What does she say to console Sylvia? What does she say which shows that she doesn't understand Sylvia? Whom and what does Mrs Groomkirby blame? What is her attitude to Sylvia?)

How does Mr Groomkirby's reaction differ from his wife's?

This extract is included under the general heading 'Of fighting of many kinds'. What is Sylvia fighting?

Discussion

In what ways can parents, school and friends help individuals to overcome their self-consciousness?

Writing

Invent a character who is particularly self-conscious about something. Write a story showing how he overcomes his self-consciousness, or fails to overcome it.

74

Improvisation

Act this extract. Continue it with Stan's arrival, and invent other characters if you wish.

Project

Find out about the Natural History Museum and the Science Museum in London. Where are they? What will you find there? If you were able to spend just an hour or so there, what would you choose to see? What preparation would you make for a visit?

The School You Would Like?

The teachers would be young and understanding, the head-mistress would be middle-aged, a wise, kind person, married, and loved by us all. She would look after us devotedly, super-vising the teachers and giving sensible advice. She would be a person with a knowledge of all subjects, a woman of the world.

GILLIAN, 13

. . . teachers that were old-fashioned would be got rid of. Old-fashioned teachers are the type that give out lines to a class that makes the slightest noise; they also regard the pupils' opinions as cheek.

RUTH, 13

Sunday Times

Give this picture a title.
Write a story or article to go with the picture. Call the story or article 'A Woman's Place is in the Home', or 'A Woman's Place is *not* in the Home'.

Write a poem or description to go with the picture. Call the poem or description 'My Sister', or 'My trouble is . . .'

Brassai

What does this picture suggest to you? Write a story or description or account of your thoughts or whatever you feel or imagine as you look at it. Give the picture a title.

'All the fun of the fair'—What *are* fairs for?

Frankie went again to the kitchen mirror and stared at her own face. 'The big mistake I made was to get this close crewcut. For the wedding I ought to have long bright yellow hair. Don't you think so?'

She stood before the mirror and she was afraid. It was the summer of fear, for Frankie, and there was one fear that could be figured in arithmetic with paper and a pencil at the table. This August she was twelve and five-sixths years old. She was five feet five and three-quarters inches tall, and she wore a number seven shoe. In the past year she had grown four inches, or at least that was what she judged. Already the hateful little summer children hollered to her: 'Is it cold up there?' And the comments of grown people made Frankie shrivel on her heels. If she reached her height on her eighteenth birthday, she had five and one-sixth growing years ahead of her. Therefore, according to mathematics and unless she could somehow stop herself, she would grow to be over nine feet tall. And what would a lady be who is over nine feet high? She would be a Freak.

In the early autumn of every year the Chattahoochee Exposition came to town. For a whole October week the fair went on down at the fair grounds. There was the Ferris Wheel, the Flying Jinney, the Palace of Mirrors – and there, too, was the House of the Freaks. The House of the Freaks was a long pavilion which was lined on the inside with a row of booths. It cost a quarter to go into the general tent, and you could look at each Freak in his booth. Then there were special private exhibitions farther back in the tent which cost a dime apiece. Frankie had seen all of the members of the Freak house last October:

The Giant
The Fat Lady
The Midget
The Pin Head
The Alligator Boy
The Half-Man Half-Woman

The Giant was more than eight feet high, with huge loose hands and a hang-jaw face. The Fat Lady sat in a chair, and the fat on her was like loose-powdered dough which she kept slapping and working with her hands – next was the squeezed Midget who minced around in little trick evening clothes. The last booth was always very crowded, for it was the booth of the Half-Man Half-Woman, a morphidite and a miracle of science. This Freak was divided completely in half – the left side was a man and the right side a woman. The costume on the left was a leopard skin and on the right a brassiere and a spangled skirt. Half the face was dark-bearded and the other half bright glazed with paint. Both eyes were strange. Frankie had wandered around the tent and looked at every booth. She was afraid of all the Freaks, for it seemed to her that they had looked at her in a secret way and tried to connect their eyes with hers, as though to say: we know you. She was afraid of their long Freak eyes. And all the year she had remembered them, until this day.

'I doubt if they ever get married or go to a wedding,' she said. 'Those Freaks.'

CARSON MCCULLERS

Questions
What was Frankie's fear?
What did Frankie work out by arithmetic?
What did the children mean when they shouted 'Is it cold up there?'
Why does Frankie remember the Freaks at the fair?

Discussion
What is adolescence?

Writing
Write a letter to a 'problem page' of a newspaper or magazine, describing (or inventing) a problem with which you need help.

Improvisation
Invent an improvisation which includes a group of adults who have forgotten or do not know the extent of a 12/13 year-old's experience and knowledge. Include a scene where some 12/13 year-olds try tactfully to bring the adults into the picture. (This improvisation will probably need a great deal of discussion and experiment before you start.)

Project
Make a tape entitled 'Adolescence'.

Columbia Pictures

What does this picture suggest to you? Write a story or description or account of your thoughts or whatever you feel or imagine as you look at it.

(What is each of the characters in the picture thinking? Is the person standing up a boy or a girl? Could it be the girl in the preceding extract, 'The summer of fear'?)

What a dandy fellow!

Lizard

A lizard ran out on a rock and looked up, listening no doubt to
the sounding of the spheres.
And what a dandy fellow! the right toss of a chin for you
and swirl of a tail!

If men were as much men as lizards are lizards
they'd be worth looking at.

D. H. LAWRENCE

Write about another 'dandy fellow'.

The School You Would Like?

My conception of an ideal school is a co-educational day school.
I see no advantage to be gained through cutting children off
from their parents and, often, from all outside affairs for most of
the year through boarding school, nor in segregating the sexes.
Schools, after all, are not only to educate but also to fit the pupil
for his life ahead, so that boarding and segregated schools which
often cause social upsets and shyness are a bad idea. It is argued
that a boarding school teaches the pupil to 'stand on his own
two feet' and to live in a community, but, in my opinion,
ordinary day school will do that equally well. The child has to
defend himself and be independent just as much, but for shorter
periods of time, which is an advantage for a sensitive person.

ALEXANDRA, 13

Youth clubs, dances, shows, societies, dramatic clubs, cinemas,
etc., in the school, held frequently, could turn it into a place of
friendship and happiness, rather than dread.

LIETTA, 12

'*I shall come to grips with the ghoul!*'

Hrothgar receives Beowulf, who announces his identity and intentions:

Hrothgar, the King of the Danes, replied to Wulfgar:

'I knew Beowulf when he was growing up, and his noble father, Ecgtheow. Now Beowulf has come to render service to a family friend. Sailors, who ferried gifts of friendship over the seas, reported that this man had the strength of thirty in his handshake and battle arm. Now the merciful God has sent him to the Danes to rid us of the toils of Grendel. I shall honour the brave man's courage with a bounty of treasure. Without further ado, welcome him to our presence to meet our noble court. Assure him also with warm words that he is welcome to the Danish people!'

Then Wulfgar returned to the entrance and pronounced the King's message: 'I am commanded to say to you by the King, that he recognizes your noble identity, and that you brave men are welcome to him over the sea surges. Now you may approach Hrothgar in all your war attire, beneath your fighting helms; but leave your shields and spear shafts here to await the outcome of your talks.'

At last then Beowulf stood up, with a circle of his men about him; commanding one section to remain to guard their weapons, Beowulf now moved swiftly into the very heart of Heorot, with the herald to guide him. Determined in his war dress and helmet, the brave visitor marched till he stood face to face with Hrothgar.

Beowulf greeted Hrothgar, his war attire gleaming, his chain mail skilfully linked by the craft of the smith: 'Peace be with you, Hrothgar! I am a high subject and kinsman of King Hygelac! I have in my youth performed many marvels. The curse of Grendel was no secret to me in Sweden. Sailors recount that this high hall, this noblest of dwellings, stands dank and deserted when the sun sets and the shadows of night-time fall. Then my friends and counsellors who knew my prowess and the strength of my arm advised my visit to your land. They witnessed my return from many a bloody battle, stained with gore. And now it is the turn of Grendel to feel the attack of my arm, as I challenge him all alone, and deal with that savager.

'But I ask of you one favour, famous King, ruler of the Danes, and now I have come this far I hope you will not deny it me: I ask that you will allow me alone, with my band of fighting men, my brave comrades, to free Heorot. Rumour also has it that this reckless beast gives no heed to weapons. Likewise, I, for the further glory of my King, Hygelac, shall forsake all swords and friendly shields. I shall come to grips with the ghoul with my bare hands, and grapple for his life, in a fight to the death.

'He who loses shall submit himself to God's judgement. I have no doubt that – if he gets the chance – Grendel will devour my warriors as he has done others in the hall of death. There will be no need to cover my head if he conquers me, for Grendel will have buried me in blood, before he carries off my remains to gorge himself on my carcass. He will be the only guest at his awful banquet as he devours my bones and lets my blood soak into the hollows of the moor. There will be no corpse for you to send out to sea with full funeral rites! If my body is destroyed in this battle, deliver to Hygelac, my King, this priceless warrior's vest which protects my breast; it is an ancestral treasure, passed down by my grandfather, the work of the world-famous Weland, the Wonderful Smith. Destiny will decree who is doomed to die!'

Hrothgar, the Danish leader, made answer to Beowulf thus: 'It pains me deeply to relate to any man the havoc that the demented Grendel has wrought for me in Heorot with his savage sorties. My companions and dear comrades in war have been decimated. Doom has delivered them for destruction by Grendel. Would that God with a touch would restrain that demon's death dealing!

'Time after time with courage found by drinking, warriors have volunteered to bide in the beer hall to tackle Grendel with their terrible twin-edged swords. Then was this mead hall, at the break of day, in the light of dawn, a scene of savage butchery with the benches drenched in blood. Thus my band diminished as death snatched them away. But now you must take your place at the feasting, and whet your appetite with tales of triumph, if you can give your mind to it!'

Then a bench was prepared in the feast house for Beowulf's

party. They took their places in due order, dauntless in their daring. A butler dutifully bore an ornamented ale-jug and decanted the clear beer. From time to time the clear-voiced minstrel's song rang in Heorot.

Unferth, one of the Danes, challenges Beowulf's ability:

Then Unferth the Restless, who sat at the feet of Hrothgar, spoke out and challenged Beowulf, because Beowulf's expedition was a thorn in his flesh: he could not suffer any man on earth to overshadow him. 'Are you the Beowulf who competed with Breca, floating around on the expanse of the sea, duelling with the deep, boasting and showing off, risking your skin on the waves? Not even your closest friends, let alone your foes, could dissuade you from your empty exploit on the sea, when you splashed about in the surf, swam up and down the coast, kicked about and floated on your back, while winter whipped up the waves. The pair of you trod water for a weary week. But Breca outswam you. He was stronger than you. So what hope will you have against Grendel, even if you dare to wait for him through the long night?'

Beowulf answered Unferth's challenge thus: 'What a lot you've had to say, in your cups, my friend! It's the beer that speaks! The truth is different that I tell! My strength in the sea and struggles with the waves are unsurpassed! When we were but growing up and still very green, Breca and I said and sealed with promises that we would try the strength of the waves, submit ourselves to the sea. That promise we honoured. When we ventured on the sea we carried a naked sword firmly in one hand, which we deemed necessary to defend ourselves against whales. As I was swifter in the sea, he could not swim far away from me in the waves, and I would not leave him. Then were we two together in the sea for the length of five nights, until the swell, the surging waters, the bitterest of weather, and the darkening night drove us apart, and the biting north wind battled abruptly against us. The waves rose in wrath, and the mood of the sea monsters turned nasty. There my body-suit, built by hand and well bonded against blows, protected me, my armoured vest, gold burnished, covered my breast. A man-eating monster suddenly seized me murderously in his clutches and dragged me down to the depths of the ocean bed. But the fortunes of the fight

84

went my way, and I drove the point of my sword deep into the horror; in the desperate dive of death my hand was the agent which did for the beast from the sea.'

Dictionary or Discussion
   decimate
   unsurpassed
   in your cups

What do you think of Unferth?

For discussion. Competitions.

Write a story about two young people who make each other an unusual promise, and carry it out.

Compose one of the songs or stories the minstrel might have sung in Heorot.

Look at the photograph on page 108.
Improvise a dance drama of Beowulf's exploits in the sea with Breca and the sea monsters.

Find out as much as you can about minstrels and make a book to illustrate 'Entertainment through the Ages'.

I (4) Of things that go bump in the night

1. *'We're on the Ark –*
   What a lark!'
2. *Bang Bang Bang*
3. *'Here they lie in enchanted sleep'*
4. *Then a new sound set up, a deathly droning. . .*

'We're on the Ark—
What a lark!'

The Ark takes aboard its last passengers:

'Thank goodness, that's over,' said Shem, as they watched the last beast pass through the door. 'Anyone else on shore?' he called; but there was no answer.

Thankfully they turned towards the door when, 'Hold hard,' said Ham, 'isn't that somebody else coming?' They listened. It was very hard to hear anything above the hiss of the rain; but surely there were footsteps coming slowly and uncertainly up the hill-side towards the Ark. Shem and Ham peered into the gloom, but nothing could be seen. Suddenly there was a loud splash. 'They've fallen down,' said Ham, with a chuckle. After a pause the steps started again: a splash, as each foot was put down, and a squelchy 'klop!' as it was pulled up again.

Then, above the edge of the little dip where the Ark lay, appeared a head, bobbing and swaying upon the sky-line; and next came shoulders and a body, with arms waving wildly now and then, to keep its balance.

'It's Mother!' said Shem and Ham in one breath, and turned and bolted for Noah. 'Father,' they shouted, 'Mother's coming!'

'Good heavens! said Noah; 'do you mean to say your mother is not on board?'

It was a very bedraggled Mrs Noah whom they saw coming up the gangway for large animals, when they got back on deck. 'Yes,' she said bitterly, 'it's about time some of you came. A nice time I've had of it.'

'My dear,' said Noah, 'we have been terribly busy getting the animals on board, and I had no idea that –'

'Where is my room?' she interrupted wearily. 'Or do I sleep with the animals?'

Noah looked very ashamed of himself. 'This way, my dear,' he answered humbly, showing her into the cabin opposite his office.

Even now it seemed that the day's work was not over; scarcely had Noah got back to his room when there came a knock at the door.

'Come in,' he said wearily. Nothing happened. 'Come in,' he repeated. Still no one appeared. 'You can come in,' he said more loudly.

'I-'m c-o-m-i-n-g,' said a slow, dragging voice.

Noah looked up. The door was opening, but so slowly that he could scarcely see it move. Presently a puffy-looking snout appeared. Then round the corner crept a quaint front paw, ending off in a kind of meat-hook, which groped slowly about until it found a bit of the floor that it could hook into. This done, the other paw arrived at the same speed.

'Do try and hurry a little,' said Noah wearily.

'A-r-e-n'-t I-I h-u-r-r-y-i-n-g a-s f-a-s-t a-s I-I c-a-n?' said the beast, without increasing its pace in the slightest.

By the time it was half-way through the door, showing a tangled, matted coat of faded brown fur, Noah felt he could wait no longer. 'You had better tell me what you want from there,' he suggested.

The beast continued slowly to lift a front leg and edge it forward, while it thought for a moment. It seemed to walk on the back of its wrists. At last its mouth began to open: 'I-'v-e n-o-w-h-e-r-e t-o s-l-e-e-p,' it drawled.

'Haven't you a cabin?' asked Noah.

'Y-e-s, b-u-t t-h-e-r-e-'s n-o-w-h-e-r-e t-o s-l-e-e-p.'

'There should be plenty of straw in it.'

'I-I c-a-n-'t s-l-e-e-p i-n s-t-r-a-w,' said this quaint beast. 'I-I m-u-s-t s-l-e-e-p r-i-g-h-t w-a-y u-p.'

'Well, then, why don't you lean against the wall and go to sleep standing up?'

'S-t-a-n-d-i-n-g u-p! B-u-t I-I m-u-s-t g-o t-o s-l-e-e-p h-a-n-g-i-n-g d-o-w-n r-i-g-h-t w-a-y u-p.'

'I don't know what you mean,' said Noah, in despair. 'You seem to be talking nonsense; but go to your cabin, and I'll get Japhet.'

'I don't know what it is,' he said to Japhet presently. 'It looks like a very old hearth-rug, and it is so slow that it makes you yawn to watch it. Here it is,' as it came slowly down the passage.

'Why, it's the Sloth!' said Japhet. 'I never saw it come on board.'

'I saw it,' said the Elephant, sticking her head out of her cabin. 'It walked up underneath the plank, and got in at a lower window. Foolhardy, I call it.'

'Oh yes,' said Japhet; 'I'd forgotten that it always lives upside down.'

'I-I d-o-n-'t k-n-o-w w-h-a-t y-o-u m-e-a-n b-y u-p-s-i-d-e d-o-w-n,' said the Sloth with some heat; 'b-u-t I-I c-a-n-'t s-l-e-e-p h-e-r-e. I-I f-e-e-l a-l-l d-i-z-z-y.'

'I don't know what's to be done for tonight,' said Japhet. 'It ought to have a rail or something to hang from.'

'There's my towel rail,' suggested the Elephant timidly.

'The very thing!' cried Noah and Japhet. Together they carried the towel rail into the other cabin. The Sloth climbed slowly up into his favourite position, hanging upside down, and almost instantly fell asleep.

Meanwhile, you must not imagine that elsewhere in the Ark everyone had fallen quietly asleep. On the contrary, there seemed to have been nothing but trouble; although it was gradually quieting down now, as one by one the animals got to sleep. . . .

In places the loud snores of heavy sleepers proved disturbing; while occasionally some timid little beast would start up from a bad dream with a shriek which woke up others. It was no better with the birds. Here the Luminous Puffins had caused an immense amount of annoyance. Shouts of 'Put that light out!', 'How can I get to sleep with that on?' filled the air; while the Owls complained bitterly that they could not see. The poor little Puffins, while very willing, were quite unable to oblige; and a deputation of birds had waited upon Noah, who at Japhet's suggestion had removed the Puffins from the birds' quarters and posted them at intervals down the passage between the animals' cabins, where they made excellent night-lights.

Little by little the various commotions died down; the complaints were satisfied, or at least stilled; and at last, all on board were asleep.

And then, from his cavern in the hills, where he dwelled in darkness, stole the loathly Scub; and slinking on board when all was still, crept unobserved into an empty cabin, and curled himself up in the darkest corner.

The Camel was the first to wake up next morning; and he could not for the life of him think where he was. It was still dark; and all he knew was that the ground he was lying on was certainly not sand. It was horribly hard, and he felt stiff and sore all over.

He scrambled to his feet, and bump! went his head against the roof of the cabin. That did it! The Camel exploded! He kicked up such a row that it was quite impossible for anyone else to remain asleep.

'For goodness' sake, shut up,' spat the Dromedary, who was in the next cabin. 'It isn't nearly time to get up yet.'

But the Camel was fairly off by now, and this only made him worse. He called the Dromedary every name he could think of – as though it was all his fault – and ended up by banging hard on the wooden partition that separated them.

'Oh, do stop that noise,' shouted someone a little farther down the passage. 'You're frightening the Elephant out of her wits. You'll have her losing her head in a minute and trampling on things.' And the animal was quite right to shout; for if an elephant loses her head and begins to trample on things it is time to get out of the way.

'Give her a melon, and tell her to remember her size,' said the Hippopotamus from a cabin opposite. All the big animals had cabins together at one end of the Ark; the middling-sized beasts were in the middle; and the smallest were at the end near where Noah and his family lived.

'Don't be silly,' said the voice. 'There aren't any melons. We are on the Ark.'

'Why, bless my soul!' said the Hippopotamus. 'So we are. I'd forgotten all about it.

> 'We're on the Ark –
> What a lark!'

And he roared with laughter, as he always did at his own jokes, however feeble.

There was no chance of any more sleep now, and even the laziest lie-a-beds found it useless to try. From every cabin came getting-up noises.

There was a big bath at the end of the passage. This was for the use of those who liked a cold bath before breakfast; and quite a lot of the animals did. Soon arose a great noise of splashing and snorting and gurgling and snuffling, followed by peals of laughter.

'Look here, we can't have the Hippopotamus and his wife in at the same time,' gasped a small Water Rat, who had been almost swamped by the waves made, as they got in together.

'Little animals should be seen and not heard,' guffawed the Hippopotamus, splashing about so that the poor little Rat was absolutely buried in spray. 'Me and Anna always has had our bath together and always shall. Now then, Anna, let's play Wumpetty-Dumps.' And the two great beasts lay down in the water and began rolling from side to side. They bumped into each other; rolled away; and then bumped again, till the other animals had to hold their sides, they were laughing so much. The little Water Rat had scrambled out as quickly as he could, and even he, annoyed as he was, could not help laughing at their clumsy antics. However, it is pretty hard work playing Wumpetty-Dumps in a bath, as you will find if you try; and at last the two of them were quite out of breath with their exertions.

'Now then, you others can try,' said the Hippopotamus, as he and his wife got out and walked off, leaving a trail of water that led right to their cabin.

KENNETH WALKER AND GEOFFREY BOUMPHREY:
The Log of the Ark

Questions
What does Mrs Noah mean when she says, 'A nice time I've had of it'?
What excuse does her husband make?

What was the Sloth's problem?
How was it solved?

What was the Owls' complaint?
How was it dealt with?

Who was last aboard?

What does 'the Camel exploded' mean?

What was the Water Rat's complaint?
How was he answered?

Discussion
The pains and pleasures of communal life.

Writing
Write a later episode in the story, involving 'the loathly Scub'.
Write a poem or song called 'We're on the Ark'.

Imagine you had been able to watch the morning antics of the animals on the Ark. Write your own description of what you might have seen. Include a detailed description of 'Wumpetty-Dumps'.

Write a description of breakfast on the first morning on the Ark, with Mrs Noah and her family. Include some of the conversation.

Write a set of rules for the Ark community.

Project
Find out as much as you can about 'the Flood'.

Tape
Write and produce a radio play, on tape, entitled 'The Arrival of the Animals'. Include in the script suggestions as to how the animals are to speak – for example, 'wearily', 'bitterly', 'in despair', and so on. Include the Sloth.

Record
Noye's Fludde by Benjamin Britten (Argo).

Bang Bang Bang

The History of the Flood

Bang Bang Bang
Said the nails in the Ark.

It's getting rather dark
Said the nails in the Ark.

For the rain is coming down
Said the nails in the Ark.

And you're all like to drown
Said the nails in the Ark.

Dark and black as sin,
Said the nails in the Ark.

So won't you all come in
Said the nails in the Ark.

But only two by two
Said the nails in the Ark.

So they came in two by two,
The elephant, the kangaroo,
And the gnu,
And the little tiny shrew.

Then the birds
Flocked in like winged words:
Two racket-tailed motmots, two macaws,
Two nut-hatches and two
Little bright robins.

And the reptiles: the gila monster, the slow-worm,
The green mamba, the cottonmouth and the alligator—
All squirmed in;

And after a very lengthy walk,
Two giant Galapagos tortoises.

And the insects in their hierarchies:
A queen ant, a king ant, a queen wasp, a king wasp,
A queen bee, a king bee,
And all the beetles, bugs, and mosquitoes,
Cascaded in like glittering, murmurous jewels.

But the fish had their wish;
For the rain came down.
People began to drown:
The wicked, the rich—
They gasped out bubbles of pure gold,
Which exhalations
Rose to the constellations.

So for forty days and forty nights
They were on the waste of waters
In those cramped quarters.
It was very dark, damp and lonely.
There was nothing to see, but only
The rain which continued to drop.
It did not stop.

So Noah sent forth a Raven. The Raven said 'Kark!
I will not go back to the Ark.'
The Raven was footloose,
He fed on the bodies of the rich—
Rich with vitamins and goo.
They had become bloated,
And everywhere they floated.
The Raven's heart was black,
He did not come back.
It was not a nice thing to do:
Which is why the Raven is a token of wrath,
And creaks like a rusty gate
When he crosses your path; and Fate
Will grant you no luck that day:
The Raven is fey:
You were meant to have a scare.

Fortunately in England
The Raven is rather rare.

Then Noah sent forth a Dove,
She did not want to rove.
She longed for her love—
The other turtle dove—
(For her no other dove!)
She brought back a twig from an olive-tree.
There is no more beautiful tree
Anywhere on the earth,
Even when it comes to birth
From six weeks under the sea.

She did not want to rove.
She wanted to take her rest,
And to build herself a nest
All in the olive grove
She wanted to make love.
She thought that was the best.

The Dove was not a rover;
So they knew that the rain was over.
Noah and his wife got out
(They had become rather stout)
And Japhet, Ham, and Shem.
(The same could be said of them.)
They looked up at the sky.
The earth was becoming dry.

Then the animals came ashore—
There were more of them than before:
There were two dogs and a litter of puppies;
There were a tom-cat and two tib-cats
And two litters of kittens—cats
Do not obey regulations;
And, as you might expect,
A quantity of rabbits.

God put a rainbow in the sky.
They wondered what it was for.

There had never been a rainbow before.
The rainbow was a sign;
It looked like a neon sign—
Seven colours arched in the skys:
What should it publicize?
They looked up with wondering eyes.

It advertises Mercy
Said the nails in the Ark.

Mercy Mercy Mercy
Said the nails in the Ark.

Our God is merciful
Said the nails in the Ark.

Merciful and gracious
Bang Bang Bang Bang.

JOHN HEATH-STUBBS

Read this poem aloud.
Invent your own History of the Flood.
Read your own poem aloud.

'Here they lie in enchanted sleep.'

Susan and Colin, on a visit to Alderley in Cheshire, hear a strange story from their host, Gowther Mossock:

The Legend of Alderley

At dawn one still October day in the long ago of the world, across the hill of Alderley, a farmer from Mobberley was riding to Macclesfield fair.

The morning was dull, but mild; light mists bedimmed his way; the woods were hushed; the day promised fine. The farmer was in good spirits, and he let his horse, a milk-white mare, set her own pace, for he wanted her to arrive fresh for the market. A rich man would walk back to Mobberley that night.

So, his mind in the town while he was yet on the hill, the farmer drew near to the place known as Thieves' Hole. And there the horse stood still and would answer to neither spur nor rein. The spur and rein she understood, and her master's stern command, but the eyes that held her were stronger than all of these.

In the middle of the path, where surely there had been no one, was an old man, tall, with long hair and beard.

'You go to sell this mare,' he said. 'I come here to buy. What is your price?'

But the farmer wished to sell only at the market, where he would have the choice of many offers, so he rudely bade the stranger quit the path and let him through, for if he stayed longer he would be late to the fair.

'Then go your way,' said the old man. 'None will buy. And I shall await you here at sunset.'

The next moment he was gone, and the farmer could not tell how or where.

The day was warm, and the tavern cool, and all who saw the mare agreed that she was a splendid animal, the pride of Cheshire, a queen among horses; and everyone said that there was no finer beast in the town. But no one offered to buy. A sour-eyed farmer rode out of Macclesfield at the end of the day.

Near Thieves' Hole the mare stopped: the stranger was there.

99

Thinking any price now better than none, the farmer agreed to sell. 'How much will you give?' he said.

'Enough. Now come with me.'

By Seven Firs and Goldenstone they went, to Stormy Point and Saddlebole. And they halted before a great rock embedded in the hill-side. The old man lifted his staff and lightly touched the rock, and it split with the noise of thunder.

At this, the farmer toppled from his plunging horse and, on his knees, begged the other to have mercy on him and let him go his way unharmed. The horse should stay; he did not want her. Only spare his life, that was enough.

The wizard, for such he was, commanded the farmer to rise. 'I promise you safe conduct,' he said. 'Do not be afraid; for living wonders you shall see here.'

Beyond the rock stood a pair of iron gates. These the wizard opened, and took the farmer and his horse down a narrow tunnel deep into the hill. A light, subdued but beautiful, marked their way. The passage ended, and they stepped into a cave, and there a wondrous sight met the farmer's eyes – a hundred and forty knights in silver armour, and by the side of all but one a milk-white mare.

'Here they lie in enchanted sleep,' said the wizard, 'until a day will come – and come it will – when England shall be in direst peril, and England's mothers weep. Then out from the hill these must ride and, in a battle thrice lost, thrice won, upon the plain, drive the enemy into the sea.'

The farmer, dumb with awe, turned with the wizard into a further cavern, and here mounds of gold and silver and precious stones lay strewn along the ground.

'Take what you can carry in payment for the horse.'

And when the farmer had crammed his pockets (ample as his lands!), his shirt, and his fists with jewels, the wizard hurried him up the long tunnel and thrust him out of the gates. The farmer stumbled, the thunder rolled, he looked, and there was only the rock above him. He was alone on the hill, near Stormy Point. The broad full moon was up, and it was night.

And although in later years he tried to find the place, neither he nor any after him ever saw the iron gates again.

ALAN GARNER: *The Weirdstone of Brisingamen*

Questions
What clues are there that the old man who stops the farmer is
no ordinary man?
What is 'safe conduct'?
When will the knights wake up, and what will they have to do?

Writing
*After hearing this legend, Susan and Colin decide to go and look for the
iron gates. They don't have any luck, and dusk is just falling when. . . .*
Continue the story from here.

Project
See if you can discover any legends attached to the area you live
in, or anywhere you know of. If you cannot discover any, invent
some. Local names or inn signs might give you some ideas. You
might be able to get some stories from people who have lived in
the area for a long time. If you can borrow a portable tape
recorder you might find it useful to record what people tell you.

Improvisation
Improvise a scene in which the children enter the cave and
discover the sleeping knights.
Devise your own method for breaking the spell.
Make a drawing of what you think the interior of the cave looks
like. Make a sketch for a stage set for this scene.

Then a new sound set up, a deathly droning . . . .

Beowulf—4

Beowulf tells of his eventual escape from the sea and its monsters. Hrothgar entrusts the Hall to Beowulf:

'I suffered sorely at the hands of the hateful sea beasts, until I dealt out some death blows as they deserved with my invaluable sword. They did not have their fill of me, those terrors, hoping to make a meal of me at their banquet at the bottom of the sea. But when morning came they were scattered slain along the shore, eaten by my sword, so in future they would not pester those who pass over the deep sea paths. Light came from the east, the bright beacon of God; the swell subsided, and I was in sight of the windswept sea walls. Fate often favours the happy-go-lucky hero! I slew nine sea monsters with my sword. Never have I heard of a harder fight in the night under the roof of heaven, nor of a man more hard put to it in the heaving ocean. Nevertheless I dodged the threatening fangs of the fiends, worn out with the struggle. The sea, the surge, the tide threw me up on to Finland's shores.

'What have you to say about that, Unferth! If you and your warriors had been prepared to fight, Grendel would not have had such an easy time of it. But when I have done with him, you will all be able to celebrate here in peace. I shall perform as I have promised, or lay down my life in this mead hall!'

Then the hall was happy, like days gone by, until the time came for slumber. Hrothgar, the King, knew well that his high hall was under constant threat from the attacker, once the sun's light waned and night blanketed all, when the shades of darkness came stalking, shapes amongst the shadows. Everyone stood up. Hrothgar exchanged courtesies with Beowulf, and wished him good fortune in the feast hall, with these words: 'Have now and hold this best of houses: make known your might, watch out for the Wrecker! Your wishes will not go unnoticed if you escape from this deadly task with your life.'

Grendel attacks Beowulf in Heorot:

So Hrothgar left the hall, and Beowulf before lying down uttered this promise: 'If Grendel comes tonight, I shall wage battle without weapons. Let him try the strength of my grip, if he dares to grace this hall with his presence while I am its guardian.' So saying, he put aside his helmet and patterned sword, and many a one of his warriors tried to sleep, though little a hope had they of finding families and homeland again.

Then there came growling, from the moors through the misty glens, Grendel himself, grim demon. He schemed to ensnare some unfortunate man in the high hall. In the darkness he sensed his way, bent on revisiting the gold adorned hall. But a surprise lay in store for him. Never in his life was he treated to such a reception from a host. Tearing down the iron-barred entrance, he invited himself in to his grisly feast, raging with flaming eyes over the tiled floor. Gurgling with greedy laughter he moved among the banquet of men, soundly asleep now and ready for eating. But it was to be Grendel's last meal of mortal men. For Beowulf was awake and secretly watching how the man-eater would go about his grim purpose. The monster was not in a mood to dally, and grabbed a sleeping man for his first course, ripped his sinews apart, crunched his joints, drank his blood, gulped it down in gouts. Soon he had gluttonously savoured the whole carcass, even the hands and feet.

He pressed on remorselessly, and stretched out to grip Beowulf next where he lay. He opened his terrible claws and reached towards the hero. But Beowulf was ready for him, and suddenly thrust himself up on his elbow, and returned the horrible handshake. Immediately it came home to Grendel that he had met his match in a grip greater than he had encountered anywhere in the world. Fear possessed him, but he could not budge from that breaking grip. His mind was fixed on flight, on escape into the unknown and the eyrie of evil he inhabited. He had met a doom more certain than he had ever sensed. Beowulf now reminded himself of the promise he had made previously. The monster's claws cracked asunder. The beast tried to pull away, but the vice grip drew him closer. Grendel's mind fixed firmly on flight to the fens; he recognized that the might of his fingers was lost in the grip of his foe. That was a sorry sortie the ravager had planned to Heorot.

The din drummed through the distinguished hall. Every Dane supped full with terror. Fury filled both contestants for the lordship of the hall. The reverberations raged so that it was a wonder that the mead hall withstood the dint of the battle. It seemed as if it would be rased to the ground. But it was fortified and strengthened within and without by iron ties, finely forged. Even so, many of the mead benches, bedecked with gold, were wrenched from their moorings. Until this day wise men had said that neither force nor treachery could destroy their splendid hall, unless fire devoured it.

Then a new sound set up, a deathly droning so that the Spear-Danes stood still within and without, each one rooted to the ground, as the demon sang his dreadful dirge of defeat, crippled with pain, bewailing his wound. He was held remorselessly by the man who was strongest in might in this life's day.

Beowulf tears off Grendel's arm; Heorot rejoices. There is a banquet to celebrate. The minstrel sings and Beowulf is honoured with gifts.

Beowulf could not let the grisly guest depart with his life, which was a menace to all men. Beowulf's comrades rallied round with their ancient swords to give what help they could. But they did not know, as they tried to seek a soft spot, that no mortal point could pierce the fiend's flesh, because he had cast a spell on all weapons that might wound him. But Beowulf still held his hand in his grip. Something had to give. Suddenly, as Grendel and Beowulf pulled in opposing directions, there was a terrible ripping and cracking and shearing as the monster's sinews tore and the arm ripped right out with the armpit. Success in battle was granted to Beowulf. Grendel, sick unto death, had to flee to the fens and seek his unhallowed home. He knew full well that the end of his life was near, his days were numbered. The Spear-Danes' wishes were fulfilled that day.

Thus did Beowulf, who had come from afar, wise and wary, fulfil his promise, rid Hrothgar's hall of its plague and put an end to its pestilence. He had good reason to be pleased with his night's work. As proof that the nightmare was now at an end, Beowulf hung Grendel's shoulder and arm and claw complete from the high roof of Heorot.

Then in the morning many a fighting man hurried to the gift hall. Folk flocked from far and near to witness the wonder, and the last of the loathsome beast. Nor did the fact that he was at death's doorway seem a sad doom to any man there who followed his tracks, – where Grendel, sick at heart and evil in mind, had dragged his dying way to the monster's mere. They saw the surface seething with blood, the welter of waves stained with gouts of gore. With death already on him, done out of his evil dreams, he lost his life in that fell fastness where hell received his heathen soul.

Then was Beowulf's fame noised abroad. Many repeated that no other man, south or north between the seas anywhere on this whole earth, was a more excellent warrior or worthy to rule. From time to time they galloped their horses in gay excitement where the paths were perfect for racing. From time to time a court minstrel, a peerless performer of tales of olden times, sang old songs, and made up a new song to celebrate Beowulf's victory. The sun shone on the high hall as Hrothgar with his queen and a majestic train of maidens entered the mead hall to greet Beowulf.

Hrothgar spoke – he stood on the high hall steps, saw the lofty ceiling adorned with gold and Grendel's relic: 'For this sight let us thank Almighty God! I have been troubled with many toils, many sorrows which I lay at Grendel's door. But God the King of Glory can perform wonder after wonder. Only recently I despaired of ever seeing an end to my sorrows while this great hall was stained with blood and beset with baleful demons. Now a warrior has, through the might of the Lord, performed a deed that all of us failed to accomplish despite all our counsels. Now I, Hrothgar, thee, Beowulf, best of men, will accept into my heart as a son. Hold highly henceforth our new relationship. Whatever you wish you shall have if it is in my power to grant. May God repay you with good luck, as He has done so far.'

Then orders were given that Heorot be quickly hung with happy decorations. Many people prepared the festive hall. The gold embroidered tapestries shone from the walls, depicting many wonderful sights to those who looked on them. Soon the hall was ready for Hrothgar. Never had such a feast been celebrated. Much mead flowed, the hall was full of friends, there was yet no hint of the treachery that Hrothulf, nephew to Hrothgar, was to work after his uncle's death. Today all toasted each other with great ceremony.

Hrothgar honoured Beowulf with a hero's gifts. He gave him a golden ensign, an ornate battle banner, a helmet, a corselet, and a jewelled sword. Beowulf's cup was full and he had no need to feel modest. He had well earned his marvellous gifts.

The helmet was particularly fine. Around the top ran a protecting rim to take the force of the blows of swords forged for fierce battle.

Hrothgar ordered that eight horses with gold-plated bridles be brought right within the hall. Upon one was a saddle, ornate and jewel bedecked, the horse-throne of Hrothgar himself. He gave all to Beowulf, and entreated him to enjoy them well. He did not stint with his gifts. He gave generous heirlooms to all Beowulf's company, and paid with gold for the life that Grendel had greedily taken.

There were songs and music, the harp was played and ballads were recited. Hrothgar's poet entertained them all with a fine old fable. The wine flowed in wonderful goblets. The rafters rang with revelry. More gifts were given to Beowulf, armlets, rings, a mantle, and the finest gold collar – as fine as the necklace of the Brisings* with its precious setting. More wine flowed. When evening came at last, Hrothgar left the hall in charge of his warriors as of old. They cleared the boards and scattered bedding on the ground. At the ready for emergency were each chief's helmet, corselet, and spear. Whatever the need, they were prepared. They were a fine people!

Dictionary or Discussion
>   gouts
>   gluttonously
>   eyrie
>   dint
>   mere
>   peerless
>   relic
>   corselet

Imagine you were one of Beowulf's warriors who witnessed the fight with Grendel and the pursuit to the mere. Describe what

---

* *Note: The Brisings* were a tribe who in ancient Norse legend made a magic necklace for a goddess called Freyja. She lost the necklace through the wickedness of an evil spirit, Loki.

you saw, in your own words. Add your own touches, if you wish. *For discussion.* 'Heaven and Hell.'

Invent the story of the treachery that is hinted at in this extract. (It might include an account of the burning of Heorot.)

Compose the ballad which the minstrel might have made up about Beowulf.

Improvise the fight between Beowulf and Grendel. (Recall your discussion on page 66.)

With the help of the comments in the extract, describe an Anglo-Saxon feast, as you imagine it.

Find out all you can about the origins of the story of Snow White and the Seven Dwarfs. Do you think this story might originally have had any connection with the *Brisings* who made the wonderful necklace? (You might like to make up a story about how Freyja came to lose the necklace, and what happened to it.)

Reading. The Weirdstone of Brisingamen by Alan Garner (Puffin).

Focus Ltd

What does this picture suggest to you?
Imagine you want two friends to pose in the exact position of these girls, so that you can take a similar photo. Describe as accurately as you can how your two friends are to pose. (Remember the details of the fingers. Guess what the girls might be pretending to be.)
What arguments would you use to support movement/dance/drama?
What arguments would you use in opposition?

II (1) Of schools and homes

1. *There were a packet of dried peas and half a bottle of vinegar on the shelves. The bread bin was empty*

2. *Be it ever so humble, there's no place like home!*

3. *It has no care*
   For gleam or gloom

4. *The headmistress was never sure which she disliked more, adolescent girls or small children*

5. *'A little, houseless match, it has no roof, no thatch,*
   It lies alone, it makes no moan, that little, houseless match.'

6. *The Home of the Monsters*

The bread bin was empty

There were no curtains up. The window was a hard-edged block the colour of the night sky. Inside the bedroom the darkness was a gritty texture. The wardrobe and bed were blurred shapes in the darkness. Silence.

Billy moved over, towards the outside of the bed. Jud moved with him, leaving one half of the bed empty. He snorted and rubbed his nose. Billy whimpered. They settled. Wind whipped the window and swept along the wall outside.

Billy turned over. Jud followed him and cough-coughed into his neck. Billy pulled the blankets up round his ears and wiped his neck with them. Most of the bed was now empty, and the unoccupied space quickly cooled. Silence. Then the alarm rang. The noise brought Billy upright, feeling for it in the darkness, eyes shut tight. Jud groaned and hutched back across the cold sheet. He reached down the side of the bed and knocked the clock over, grabbed for it, and knocked it farther away.

'Come here, you bloody thing.'

He stretched down and grabbed it with both hands. The glass lay curved in one palm, while the fingers of his other hand fumbled amongst the knobs and levers at the back. He found the lever and the noise stopped. Then he coiled back into bed and left the clock lying on its back.

'The bloody thing.'

He stayed in his own half of the bed, groaning and turning over every few minutes, Billy lay with his back to him, listening. Then he turned his cheek slightly from the pillow.

'Jud?'

'What?'

'Tha'd better get up.'

No answer.

'Alarm's gone off tha knows.'

'Think I don't know?'

He pulled the blankets tighter and drilled his head into the pillow. They both lay still.

'Jud?'

'What?'

'Tha'll be late.'

'O, shut it.'

'Clock's not fast tha knows.'

'I said SHUT IT.'

He swung his fist under the blankets and thumped Billy in the kidneys.

'Gi'o'er! That hurts!'

'Well shut it then.'

'I'll tell my mam on thi.'

Jud swung again. Billy scuffled away into the cold at the edge of the bed, sobbing. Jud got out, sat on the edge of the bed for a moment, then stood up and felt his way across the room to the light switch. Billy worked his way back to the centre and disappeared under the blankets.

'Set t'alarm for me, Jud. For seven.'

'Set it thi sen.'

'Go on, tha'r up.'

Jud parted Billy's sweater and shirt, and used the sweater for a vest. Billy snuggled down in Jud's place, making the springs creak. Jud looked at the humped blankets, then walked across and pulled them back, stripping the bed completely.

Jud went downstairs. Billy sat on the edge of the bed and re-set the alarm, then ran across the lino and switched the light off. When he got back into bed most of the warmth had gone. He shivered and scuffled around the sheet, seeking a warm place.

It was still dark outside when he got up and went downstairs. The living-room curtains were drawn, and when he switched the light on it was gloomy and cold without the help of the fire. He placed the clock on the mantelpiece, then picked up his mother's sweater from the settee and pulled it on over his shirt.

The alarm rang as he was emptying the ashes in the dustbin. Dust clouded up into his face as he dropped the lid back on and ran inside, but the noise stopped before he could reach it. He knelt down in front of the empty grate and scrunched sheets of newspaper into loose balls, arranging them in the grate like a bouquet of hydrangea flowers. Then he picked up the hatchet, stood a nog of wood on the hearth and struck it down the centre. The blade bit and held. He lifted the hatchet with the nog attached and smashed it down, splitting the nog in half and chipping the tile with the blade. He split the halves into quarters down through eighths to sixteenths, then arranged these sticks over the paper like the struts of a wigwam. He completed the construction with lumps of coal, building them into a loose shell, so that sticks and paper showed through the chinks. The paper caught with the first match, and the flames spread quickly underneath, making the chinks smoke and the sticks crack. He waited for the first burst of flames up the back of the construction, then stood up and walked into the kitchen, and opened the pantry door. There were a packet of dried peas and a half bottle of vinegar on the shelves. The bread bin was empty. Just inside the doorway, the disc of the electricity meter circled slowly in its glass case. The red arrow appeared, and disappeared. Billy closed the door and opened the outside door. On the step stood two empty milk bottles. He thumped the jamb with the side of his fist.

'It's t' same every morning. I'm going to start hiding some at nights.'

BARRY HINES: *A Kestrel for a Knave*

Questions
What kind of person is Billy? Do you like him?
What kind of person is Jud? Do you like him?
From the information in the extract, describe Billy's home and the atmosphere in it.

For discussion
Swearing.
The early bird catches the worm.

Writing
'The Alarm Clock.'
'Getting up in the Morning.'
'My Brother (or Sister).' (If you haven't got one, invent one.)
'Home, Sweet Home.'

Film
Kes.

'Be it ever so humble, there's no place like home!'

Home, Sweet Home!

'Mid pleasures and palaces though we may roam,
Be it ever so humble, there's no place like home!
A charm from the skies seems to hallow us there,
Which, seek through the world, ne'er is met with elsewhere.

Home! home! sweet, sweet home!
There's no place like home, there's no place like home!

An exile from home, splendour dazzles in vain,
O give me my lovely thatched cottage again!
The birds singing gaily, that came at my call,
Give me them, with the peace of mind, dearer than all.

Home! home! sweet, sweet home!
There's no place like home, there's no place like home!

JOHN HOWARD PAYNE

Questions
What do you think of this song?
Is it a song which Billy, in the previous extract, might sing?
What, would you say, are the essential things which make 'a home'?
Write your own song or poem about Home.

The music of this song was written by Henry Rowley Bishop. See if you can find out anything about him, and the origin of the song.

The following is taken from a United States newspaper of October 1935:
'At Lawton, Oklahoma, John Brett, an attorney, sang "Home, Sweet Home" to a jury so as to induce clemency for his client Lloyd Grable, a bank robber. The jury responded with a verdict of life imprisonment for Mr Grable.'
What is an attorney? Why, do you think, did he sing 'Home, Sweet Home'? Did it make any difference to the result?

114

What does this picture suggest to you? Write a story or description or account of your thoughts or whatever you feel or imagine as you look at it.

It has no care
For gleam or gloom

Gone the wild day:
A wilder night
Coming makes way
For brief twilight.

Where the firm soaked road
Mounts and is lost
In the high beech-wood
It shines almost.

The beeches keep
A stormy rest,
Breathing deep
Of wind from the west.

The wood is black,
With a misty steam.
Above, the cloud pack
Breaks for one gleam.

But the woodman's cot
By the ivied trees
Awakens not
To light or breeze.

It smokes aloft
Unwavering:
It hunches soft
Under storm's wing.

It has no care
For gleam or gloom:
It stays there
While I shall roam,

Die, and forget
The hill of trees,
The gleam, the wet,
This roaring peace.

EDWARD THOMAS: *Interval*

Write your own poem called 'This roaring peace'.

*The headmistress was never sure which she disliked
more . . .*

It was about three o'clock on a Friday afternoon when Annette
decided to leave school. . . . I am learning nothing here, she
thought. From now on I shall educate myself. I shall enter the
School of Life. She packed her books up neatly and rose. She
crossed the room, bowing gravely to the tutor, who had interrupted her reading and was looking at Annette with disapproval.
Annette left the room, closing the door quietly behind her. When
she found herself outside in the heavily carpeted corridor, she
began to laugh. It was all so absurdly simple, she could not
imagine why she had not thought of it long ago. She crossed the
corridor with a skip and a jump, making a tasteful vase of
flowers rock upon its pedestal, and went down the steps to the
cloakroom three at a time. . . .

Annette was nearly nineteen. Concerning Ringenhall she
herself had not experienced a single moment of doubt. She had
loathed it from the very first day. For her fellow-pupils she felt
a mixture of pity and contempt, and for her teachers, who were
called 'tutors', contempt unmixed. For the headmistress, a Miss
Walpole, she felt a pure and disinterested hatred. 'Disinterested',
because Miss Walpole had never behaved unpleasantly to
Annette or indeed paid any attention to her whatsoever.
Annette had never hated anyone in this way before and took
pride in the emotion, which she felt to be a sign of maturity. . . .
When it was possible, she read a book or wrote letters in class.
When this was not possible, she pursued some lively daydream,
or else fell into a self-induced coma of stupidity. To do this she
would let her jaw fall open and concentrate her attention upon
some object in the near vicinity until her eyes glazed and there
was not a thought in her head. After some time, however, she
discontinued this practice, not because the tutors began to think
that she was not right in the head – this merely amused her – but
because she discovered that she was able by this means to make
herself fall asleep, and this frightened her very much indeed.

Annette put her coat on and was ready to go. But now when
she reached the door that led into the street she paused suddenly.
She turned round and looked along the corridor. Everything

seemed the same; the expensive flora, the watery reproductions of famous paintings, the much admired curve of the white staircase. Annette stared at it all. It looked to her the same, and yet different. It was as if she had walked through the looking-glass. She realized that she was free. . . .

She looked about her. Ringenhall was at her mercy.

There were things which Annette had wanted very much to do ever since she had arrived. . . She had always wanted to swing on the chandelier in the dining-room. She turned rapidly in the direction of that room and bounded in. Tables and chairs stood by, silent with disapproval. Annette looked up at the chandelier and her heart beat violently. The thing seemed enormously high up and far away. It hung from a stout chain; Annette had noticed this carefully when she had studied it in the past. She had also remarked a strong metal bar, right in the centre of it, on which she had always planned to put her hands. All about and above this bar were suspended tiny drops of crystal, each one glowing with a drop of pure light tinier still, as if a beautiful wave had been arrested in the act of breaking while the sun was shining upon it. Annette had felt sure that if she could swing upon the chandelier the music which was hidden in the crystals would break out into a great peal of bells. But now it seemed to be very hard to get at.

In her imagination Annette had always reached her objective by a flying leap from the High Table; but she could see now that this was not a very practical idea. Grimly she began to pull one of the tables into the centre of the room. On top of the table she placed one of the chairs. Then she began to climb up. By the time she was on the table she was already beginning to feel rather far away from the ground. Annette was afraid of heights. However, she mounted resolutely on to the chair. Here, by standing on tiptoe, she could get her hands over the metal bar. She paused breathlessly. Then with a quick movement she kicked the chair away and hung stiffly in mid-air. The chandelier felt firm, her grip' was strong, there was no terrible rending sound as the chain parted company with the ceiling. After all, thought Annette, I don't weigh much.

She kept her feet neatly together and her toes pointed. Then with an oscillation from the hips she began to swing very gently to and fro. The chandelier began to ring, not with a deafening peal but with a very high and sweet tinkling sound; the sort of sound, after all, which you would expect a wave of the sea to make if it had been immobilized and turned into glass: a tiny internal rippling, a mixture of sound and light. Annette was completely enchanted by this noise and by the quiet rhythm of her own movements. She fell into a sort of trance, and as she swung dreamily to and fro she had a vision of remaining there for the rest of the afternoon until the boarders of Ringenhall, streaming in for their dinner, would make their way round on either side of her swinging feet and sit down, paying her no attention than if she had been a piece of furniture.

At that moment the door opened and Miss Walpole came in. Annette, who was at the end of one of her swings, let go abruptly of the chandelier and, missing the table, fell to the floor with a crash at Miss Walpole's feet. Miss Walpole looked down at her with a slight frown. This lady was never sure which she disliked more, adolescent girls or small children; the latter made more noise, it was true, but they were often in the long run easier to handle.

'Get up, Miss Cockeyne,' she said to Annette in her usual weary tone of voice. She always sighed when she spoke, as if wearied; and as she never cared particularly about anything, so nothing much ever surprised her. This calm indifference had won her the reputation of being a good headmistress.

Annette got up, rubbing herself. It has been a painful fall. Then she turned and put the table straight, and picked up the chair, which was lying on its side. After that, she retrieved her coat and bag and faced Miss Walpole.

'What were you doing, Miss Cockeyne?' asked Miss Walpole, sighing.

'Swinging from the chandelier,' said Annette. She was not afraid of her headmistress, whose claims to moral or intellectual excellence she had seen through some time ago.

'Why?' asked Miss Walpole.

Annette had no ready answer to this, and thought she might as well skip a point or two in the conversation by saying immediately, 'I'm sorry.' Then she said, 'I've decided to leave Ringenhall.'

'May I again ask why?' asked Miss Walpole.

She was an extremely tall woman, which was also perhaps one of the secrets of her success, and although Annette, too, was tall, she had to throw her head back if she wanted to look into

Miss Walpole's eyes. Annette took a step or two away and receded until the line which joined her eyes to Miss Walpole's made a nearer approach to the horizontal. She wanted to look dignified. But as she moved away, Miss Walpole imperceptibly approached, gliding forward as if propelled from behind, so that Annette had once more to crane her neck.

'I have learnt all that I can learn here,' said Annette. 'From now on I shall educate myself. I shall go out into the School of Life.'

'As to your having learnt all that you can learn here,' said Miss Walpole, 'that is clearly untrue. . . . As I had occasion to remark the other day, you still go upstairs on all fours like a dog.'

'I mean,' said Annette, 'that I've learnt all the things which I consider important.'

'What makes you imagine,' said Miss Walpole, 'that anything of *importance* can be taught in a school?' She sighed again. 'You realize, I suppose,' she went on, 'that your parents have paid in advance for tuition and meals up to the end of next term, and there can be no question of refunding that money?'

'It doesn't matter,' said Annette.

'You are fortunate to be able to say so,' said Miss Walpole. 'As for the institution which you call the School of Life, I doubt, if I may venture a personal opinion, whether you are yet qualified to benefit from its curriculum. . . . Remember that the secret of all learning is patience and that curiosity is not the same thing as a thirst for knowledge. Also remember that I am always here.'

Annette, who had no intention of imprinting this disagreeable idea on her mind, said, 'Thank you,' and backed away rapidly towards the door. In a moment she was hurrying down the corridor and jumping into the street.

As soon as Annette found herself outside, she began to run. This was not because she wanted to get away from Ringenhall Ladies' College but because whenever she was feeling pleased and excited she would run. . . . Annette wore underneath her dress two or three coloured petticoats; so that as she ran, and as the April wind now did its best to sweep her from the ground, her long legs appeared in a kaleidoscope of whirling colours.

IRIS MURDOCH: *The Flight from the Enchanter*

Questions
Why does Annette decide to leave school?
What does she do before she leaves the school?
What do you think of Annette?
What do you think of Miss Walpole?
What would *you* have said to Annette if you had been the head-mistress?
What arguments does Miss Walpole use to put Annette off leaving?

Discussion
Can 'anything of *importance*' be taught in school?
(What does Miss Walpole mean when she asks Annette, 'What makes you imagine that anything of *importance* can be taught in a school?')

Writing
Write a letter, as from Miss Walpole, to Annette's parents.
Write a letter, as from Annette, to her parents, telling them what has happened and what she proposes to do.
Write a story called 'The School of Life'.

'A little, houseless match, it has no roof, no thatch'

The narrator describes how she spent Christmas at Linda's:

There was a tremendous scraping of chairs as I came in, and a pack of Radletts hurled themselves upon me with the intensity and almost the ferocity of a pack of hounds hurling itself upon a fox. All except Linda. She was the most pleased to see me, but determined not to show it. When the din had quieted down and I was seated before a scone and a cup of tea, she said:

'Where's Brenda?' Brenda was my white mouse.

'She got a sore back and died,' I said. Aunt Sadie looked anxiously at Linda.

'Had you been riding her?' said Louisa, facetiously.

Enormous tears were pouring into Linda's plate. Nobody cried so much or so often as she; anything, but especially anything sad about animals, would set her off, and, once begun, it was a job to stop her. She was a delicate, as well as a highly nervous child, and even Aunt Sadie, who lived in a dream as far as the health of her children was concerned, was aware that too much crying kept her awake at night, put her off her food, and did her harm. The other children, and especially Louisa and Bob, who loved to tease, went as far as they dared with her, and were periodically punished for making her cry.

Wicked Louisa had invented a poem which never failed to induce rivers of tears:

'A little, houseless match, it has no roof, no thatch,

It lies alone, it makes no moan, that little houseless match.'

When Aunt Sadie was not around the children would chant this in a gloomy chorus. In certain moods one had only to glance at a match-box to dissolve poor Linda; when, however, she was feeling stronger, more fit to cope with life, this sort of teasing would force out of her very stomach an unwilling guffaw. Linda was not only my favourite cousin, but, then and for many years, my favourite human being.

I could see that she was really minding much more about Brenda than I did. The truth was that my honeymoon days with the mouse were long since over; we had settled down to an uninspiring relationship, a form, as it were, of married blight, and, when she had developed a disgusting sore patch on her back, it had been all I could do to behave decently and treat her with common humanity. Apart from the shock it always is to find somebody stiff and cold in their cage in the morning, it had been a very great relief to me when Brenda's sufferings finally came to an end.

'Where is she buried?' Linda muttered furiously, looking at her plate

'Beside the robin. She's got a dear little cross and her coffin was lined with pink satin.'

'Now, Linda darling,' said Aunt Sadie, 'if Fanny has finished her tea why don't you show her your toad?'

'He's upstairs asleep,' said Linda. But she stopped crying.

'Have some nice hot toast, then.'

'Can I have Gentleman's Relish on it?' she said, quick to make capital out of Aunt Sadie's mood, for Gentleman's Relish was kept strictly for Uncle Matthew, and supposed not to be good for children. The others made a great show of exchanging significant looks. These were intercepted, as they were meant to be, by Linda, who gave a tremendous bellowing boo-hoo and rushed upstairs.

'I wish you children wouldn't tease Linda,' said Aunt Sadie, irritated out of her usual gentleness, and followed her.

The staircase led out of the hall. When Aunt Sadie was beyond earshot, Louisa said: 'If wishes were horses beggars would ride. Child hunt tomorrow, Fanny.'

'Yes, Josh told me. He was in the car – been to see the vet.'

My Uncle Matthew had four magnificent bloodhounds, with which he used to hunt his children. Two of us would go off with a good start to lay the trail, and Uncle Matthew and the rest would follow the hounds on horseback. It was great fun. Once he came to my home and hunted Linda and me over Shenley Common. This caused the most tremendous stir locally, the Kentish week-enders on their way to church were appalled by the sight of four great hounds in full cry after two little girls. My uncle seemed to them like a wicked lord of fiction, and I became more than ever surrounded with an aura of madness, badness, and dangerousness for their children to know.

The child hunt on the first day of this Christmas visit was a great success. Louisa and I were chosen as hares. We ran across country, the beautiful bleak Cotswold uplands, starting soon after breakfast when the sun was still a red globe, hardly over the horizon, and the trees were etched in dark blue against a pale blue, mauve, and pinkish sky. The sun rose as we stumbled on, longing for our second wind; it shone, and there dawned a beautiful day, more like late autumn in its feeling than Christmas-time.

We managed to check the bloodhounds once by running through a flock of sheep, but Uncle Matthew soon got them on the scent again, and, after about two hours of hard running on our part, when we were only half a mile from home, the baying slavering creatures caught up with us, to be rewarded with lumps of meat and many caresses. Uncle Matthew was in a radiantly good temper, he got off his horse and walked home with us, chatting agreeably. What was most unusual, he was even quite affable to me.

'I hear Brenda has died,' he said. 'No great loss I should say. That mouse stank like merry hell. I expect you kept her cage too near the radiator. I always told you it was unhealthy, or did she die of old age?'

Uncle Matthew's charm, when he chose to turn it on, was considerable, but at that time I was always mortally afraid of him, and made the mistake of letting him see that I was.

'You ought to have a dormouse, Fanny, or a rat. They are much more interesting than white mice – though I must frankly say, of all the mice I ever knew, Brenda was the most utterly dismal.'

'She was dull,' I said, sycophantically.

'When I go to London after Christmas, I'll get you a dormouse. Saw one the other day at the Army & Navy.'

'Oh Fa, it *is* unfair,' said Linda, who was walking her pony along beside us. 'You know how I've always longed for a dormouse.'

'It is unfair' was a perpetual cry of the Radletts when young. The great advantage of living in a large family is that early lesson of life's essential unfairness.

NANCY MITFORD: *The Pursuit of Love*

Questions
Why would glancing at a match-box sometimes 'dissolve poor Linda'?
Why did Uncle Matthew seem like 'a wicked lord of fiction'?

What do you think of Aunt Sadie?
What do you think of Linda?
What do you think of the narrator?

Writing
Write a story where Billy (see page 111) meets Linda and her family.
Imagine you watched the Christmas 'hunt'. Write a letter to someone you know saying what you saw. (Make it clear whether the person you are writing to is a relation, a close or distant friend, an acquaintance, or perhaps someone you do not know.)

Discussion
Do you think that life is unfair? Is this one of the lessons of life? Is it an advantage to come from a home where there are a lot of children? Are there advantages in belonging to a small family?

Project
Imagine that Annette from the earlier extract (page 117) inherits some money and decides to start her own ideal school. Billy, Linda, Fanny, and other characters you have met in this book, or whom you invent, become pupils at the school. Plan the outline of the story of the school, its pupils and staff, their successes and failures. Write some of the chapters of the book. (How is the school organized and run? What is the curriculum? Is it a 'resident' school?)

Improvisation
Imagine that Fanny plucks up courage, gets Linda's toad, and puts it in Uncle Matthew's bed.
Improvise the conversation and action leading up to this; Uncle Matthew's discovery of the toad; the scene and conversation next morning at breakfast.

The School You Would Like?
The school I'd like is what I have: my mother teaches my brother and me at home. We study maths, English, science, history, geography, French and scripture.

This system has many advantages. The most important is that we can learn at our own speed; thus I have recently started A-level maths but am still struggling with O English, while my brother, who is three and a half years younger, is advanced in English but only average in arithmetic. Another advantage is that we have much more free time than other children; we don't waste time travelling to and fro and, as we have individual work, the education officer agreed to shorten lesson times for us. I spend a lot of my leisure time reading, bird watching, stamp and coin collecting, doing jigsaws, carpentry, painting, listening to radio, watching TV, swimming, playing chess, draughts, tennis and table tennis. Another advantage is that we are not hedged in by a lot of silly rules and regulations. We are also free from bullying big boys and from pressure to start bad habits like smoking and drug taking. We dress in comfortable, sensible clothes and do not have to wear some ridiculous uniform, nor do we have to play compulsory games. Again, we have home cooking all the time.

When my mother started, a lot of people told her she was foolish because we would never learn to mix. I don't think this is true because, although I've always liked some time by myself, my brother likes and has lots of friends with whom he goes to play and who come and play with him. . . . It was also said that we would grow up selfish: I hope we're not. About once a fortnight we have a stall in our front garden to aid Oxfam and have collected £4.11 so far this year. We also do a few odd jobs around the house. People also said Mother would find it too much. I know we get her down at times, but she survives and looks, so people say, much younger than she is. . . .

The only disadvantage of the system to my mind is the difficulty of doing much advanced practical work in science because of the amount of apparatus required. . . .

I think it would solve a lot of problems if more people followed our system. Of course, not everyone is qualified to teach older children, but millions of mums could teach juniors. This would reduce the terrible overcrowding in some primary schools. Again, as children would be home for longer, it might help to decrease the birth rate.

FRANK, 12

Perhaps in the not-so-distant future, man's intelligence will have improved so much that children will be able to be taught by their parents in the home.

JENNIFER, 13

Discussion
Discuss the views expressed by Frank and Jennifer.

Writing
The school *I'd* like.

Adlard

Give this picture a title.
Write a story, or poem, or an account of your thoughts and feelings as you look at it.
(If you wish, you can tell the story as if you were the owl.)

Beowulf—5

So they fell asleep. One paid a heavy price for his evening's rest, just as they used to when Grendel worried the gold-hall and took his toll, until his fate overtook him and he paid his life for his badness. It became very clear that an avenger survived that battle, bent on revenge. Grendel's dam, the female of the ghastly species who had given birth to the beast, brooded over her bereavement. She was doomed to dwell in the wastes of water, the chilling currents of the tarn, because the seed of evil was sown in her soul. Hungry and hateful, while the Spear-Danes slept soundly, she set off on an evil expedition to the high hall to take revenge for the death blow dealt to her son. She arrived at Heorot while the Danes were fast asleep in the happy festive hall.

The entrance of Grendel's mother soon changed all that. Swords were seized and shields upraised where they had been laid at the ready. But facing the female's fury they forgot their helmets and corselets. She wanted to waste no time but to get out safe and sound when she had been spotted. She fixed her fangs firmly into the first warrior in her way, a well-beloved hero, and made off to the fens, snatching Grendel's bloody claw as she went. Where was Beowulf? He had been given other quarters after the banquet. Horror reigned again in Heorot. Hrothgar was downcast to have suffered the death of another dear counsellor. Quickly Beowulf was brought to the King's bed-chamber, at break of day, wondering whether there would ever be a change of fortune, with these constant bad tidings. The rafters rang as he crossed the chamber with his companions. He asked Hrothgar how the night had been.

King Hrothgar replied: 'Do not demand to know how the night has been. Dead is Aeschere, my trusted adviser and comrade. Some woeful, wandering horror in Heorot has wreaked vengeance on his life. I do not know where the baleful beast bore his lifeless body. She has taken revenge because last night you slew Grendel by the force of your hand, since he had for too long harassed and harried my people to death. He forfeited his life and now another great scourge has come to avenge her evil offspring.

'I have heard it rumoured by great and small that they have seen two such mighty marsh creatures, evil demons, haunting the moors; one of these two creatures, as far as they could tell, resembled a woman; the other, whom folk in former days named "Grendel", roamed the wilderness masquerading as a man, though he dwarfed any human being alive; they are the ancestors of demons. They haunt the hidden land, the wolf-infested fells, the windswept crags, fearful fen tracks, where falling forests dissolve into mist and disappear below ground. It is not many milestones from here that the monsters' mere is to be found, overshadowed with wintry undergrowth, the water entangled with the twisted deep roots. There you may witness each night the seering spectre of flames darting from the flood water. No human being alive has plumbed the unknown depths. Though the heath-stalker hard pressed by the hounds, the hart hardy with high antlers might seek the sanctuary of the wood pursued from afar, he will sacrifice his life and be torn to pieces on the brink rather than attempt to escape in those waters. It is no place to linger. The troubled waves toss themselves up threateningly to the lowering sky when the wind calls up terrifying tempests, the light fails and the heavens dissolve in floods. Now again it is to you alone, Beowulf, we turn for consolation. As yet you do not know the lair of the monster where you might seek her out, if you have the heart. If you return safely, I will heap heirlooms on you as before, twisted gold for the greatest of debts.'

Beowulf replied: 'Be comforted, man of wisdom! It is better to seek revenge for a friend than to grieve too much. Each of us must abide an end to this world's life. Let each one who can, win fame before death, because that is the surest way to survival. Arise, protector of your people, let us use the time with speed to survey the scene and track down Grendel's kinswoman. I promise you she shall not lose us, go where she will, whether she choose the bosom of the earth, the fastness of the forest, or the infinite depth of the sea. Accept this consolation, as I know you will, for all your woes this day.'

Hrothgar sprang up and gave thanks to God for Beowulf's promise. A horse was made ready for Hrothgar, with bridle and plaited main. The wise prince went forward ceremoniously, with the shielded infantry. The tracks were easily discernible through the dense woods and over the marsh ground. With Aeschere's body she had made straight for the sanctuary of her watery abode. The pursuers followed over the steep slopes, the narrow niches, the cramped solitary paths, secret ways, beetling crags and lairs of water demons. Hrothgar forged ahead with a few experienced troops to reconnoitre, until he suddenly fell upon a grey grove of forest shading a dismal quarry. The waters rippled below, troubled and bloodstained.

The evil sight enveloped the Danes with anger and grief – Aeschere's head lay aslant a crag overlooking the mere. While they watched the waters churned with gore. From time to time the trumpet sounded eagerly. As the warriors took their rest, the waters swarmed with reptiles and water dragons infesting the depths. Water snakes and monsters slithered over the slopes. The war horn frightened them off, enraged. One was transfixed by Hrothgar's arrow and struggled vainly, as its fatal wound weakened it in the waves. The beast's death was speeded by the flurry of boar spears which followed the arrow when the creature began to flag. When it had given up the ghost the warriors dragged it on to the edge and examined it in horror.

Beowulf clad himself in his corselet, not afraid even to lose his life. The skill of the weaver of that armoured vest was soon to be tested in the waters of the mere. The gleaming helmet protected his head. Adorned with gold, hooped with broad bands, decorated with boars, fortified by the ancient armourer to be proof against all battle blows, the helmet was soon to plunge into the depths below and weave its way down through the whirlpool of waters. And Unferth lent Beowulf in his need the ancient sword, Hrunting, whose iron blade was adorned with deadly twig-like patternings and tempered by the blood of battle. It had never failed any man in time of need on any perilous venture. Beowulf was ready and fearless of the fray.

Dictionary or Discussion
  dam
  bereavement
  tarn
  wreaked vengeance
  scourge

masquerading
hart
lowering sky
discernible

It is sometimes said that the exploits of Beowulf are like a fairy tale – but the people in the story are not like people in fairy tales. What do you think of the people in Beowulf? What do they believe in? What do they value? What do they regard as the qualities of a hero? What kind of things do they say about life and how to live it?

For discussion. 'Each of us must abide an end to this world's life.'

Look at the Sutton Hoo helmet on page 134. Sketch it. How does it compare with the helmet Beowulf wears to venture into the mere against Grendel's mother?

Invent a game which includes heroes competing to find a treasure hoard and save a damsel in distress. You might put various dragons and monsters in the heroes' way. If you like, use a game like Snakes and Ladders, or Monopoly, to give you some ideas.

Compose a poem which describes the home of a twentieth-century monster.

Draw a strip cartoon depicting the events in this extract. Under each cartoon, say briefly what is happening.

Make up a play or write a story called 'Tit-for-Tat', or 'I'll get my revenge!'

Film. Hamlet.

Reading. Find an account of the seven labours of Hercules.

© BBC 'Living Language'. John Freeman

What does this picture suggest to you? Write a story or description or account of your thoughts or whatever you feel or imagine as you look at it.
(Who is the man? What is he doing? What happens?)

These pictures show the front and side views of the same helmet. From what you can see in the two pictures, describe the helmet in as much detail and as accurately as you can.

Tell a story about the helmet. If you wish, you could let the helmet tell its own story. Or you could tell the story of the man or men who wore it. Include yourself in the story if you wish.

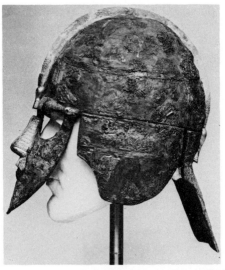

© British Museum, Sutton Hoo provisional guide

II (2) **Of Mothers and Fathers**

1. *All mothers can serve up a bit of buttered toast*
2. *'Promise not to tell father'*
3. *'Too late : my father was upon us'*
4. *'Don't tell your mother'*
5. *'Tell your mother as 'er mester's*
   Got hurt i' th' pit –'
6. *'If death should carry me off, do the duties of a father'*

I know one thing that I would make a rule, it's to have all the teachers meet our mothers at school, only if it's once a term it would be the best thing which ever happened.

K. (boy), 13

I attend what is known as a direct grant school, which is in my opinion a public school which has fallen into bad times and is helped by the government. In fact it is run like this with the bourgeois air of a public school. It has a high academic standard and a highly trained staff headed by an excellent but maybe disliked headmistress. The school is in beautiful surroundings with good facilities for work, the arts and sport. It sounds like the dream school, may be, but its outside looks are deceptive. . . .

MONICA, 14

All mothers can serve up a bit of buttered toast

My Mother

All mothers can serve up a bit of buttered toast,
Most mothers can handle a pie or a roast,
A few can boil a shark à la Barbary Coast,
But when I say mine can COOK – it's no boast.

When the Maharajah of old Srinigar
Wishes to make himself popular
Who can help him out but my Ma?
With elephant loads of nuts and suet,
With hundreds of coolies to trample through it
(To stir it you see), she produces a Cake
As huge as a palace that architects make –
Frosted and crusted with pink and blue icing.
Oh think of the knife they need for the slicing!

But special dishes are more to her wishes –
Nutritious, delicious, peculiar dishes –
Not just kippers in carrot juice,
But Buffalo Puff and Whipped-Cream Goose,
A Bouillabaisse out of no cook-book pages
With Whale and Walrus in collops and wedges
And festoons of Octopus over the edges.
(And should that give you the slightest uneasiness
There's Rose Crush topped with a peach's fleeciness.)

Sautéed Ant Eggs on Champagne Alligator
Are wonderful with a baked potato!
I took her a rattlesnake that had attacked us:
She served it up curried with Crème de la Cactus.
Her kitchen is a continual crisis,
Billowing clouds of aromas and spices –
Bubbling cauldrons and humming ovens,
Pans spitting by sixes, pots steaming by sevens.

Most mothers stick to their little cook-books,
But this is the way *my* Mother cooks!

TED HUGHES: *Meet My Folks!*

Questions
What would you expect to find on the menu if you went for a meal with the mother Ted Hughes writes about?

Discussion
Slimming. (Make a calory chart.)

Projects
Find out what you can about nutrition. What food does man need to live? How much does he need? What is bad for him? What would a person mean who warned another, 'Watch out you don't dig your grave with your teeth!'
Make a visit to a café which specializes in food which is not English. (It might be Indian or Chinese.) In what ways is the food different from the food you are used to? Can you suggest why it is different?

Writing
My favourite food.
Write a menu for your ideal meal.
A recipe for a dish you particularly enjoy.

Improvisation
Eat your way (in mime) through a meal prepared by Ted Hughes's mother.

Black and White; Andrei Punsuh

Give this picture a title.
Write a poem or song or an account of your thoughts and feelings as you look at it.
Write a story called 'How I (or my mother, or sister, or brother, or anyone you choose) got my (or her or his) wings'.
Is this your idea of a fairy?
What would you do if you found a fairy in your kitchen?

'Promise not to tell father'

Mother and Son

Although it was only five o'clock, the sun had already set and the evening was very still, as all spring evenings are, just before the birds begin to sing themselves to sleep; or maybe tell one another bedside stories. The village was quiet. The men had gone away to fish for the night after working all the morning with the sowing. Women were away milking the cows in the little fields among the crags.

Brigid Gill was alone in her cottage waiting for her son to come home from school. He was now an hour late, and as he was only nine she was very nervous about him especially as he was her only child and he was a wild boy always getting into mischief, mitching from school, fishing minnows on Sunday and building stone 'castles' in the great crag above the village. She kept telling herself that she would give him a good scolding and beating when he came in, but at the same time her heart was thumping with anxiety and she started at every sound, rushing out to the door and looking down the winding road, that was now dim with the shadows of the evening. So many things could happen to a little boy.

His dinner of dried fish and roast potatoes was being kept warm in the oven among the peat ashes beside the fire on the hearth, and on the table there was a plate, a knife and a little mug full of buttermilk.

At last she heard the glad cries of the schoolboys afar off, and rushing out she saw them scampering, not up the road, but across the crags to the left, their caps in their hands.

'Thank God,' she said, and then she persuaded herself that she was very angry. Hurriedly she got a small dried willow rod, sat down on a chair within the door and waited for Stephen.

He advanced up the yard very slowly, walking near the stone fence that bounded the vegetable garden, holding his satchel in his left hand by his side, with his cap in his right hand, a red-cheeked slim boy, dressed in close-fitting grey frieze trousers that reached a little below his knees and a blue sweater. His feet were bare and covered with all sorts of mud. His face perspired and his great soft blue eyes were popping out of his head with fright. He knew his mother would be angry.

At last he reached the door and, holding down his head, he entered the kitchen. The mother immediately jumped up and seized him by the shoulder. The boy screamed, dropped his satchel and his cap and clung to her apron. The mother raised the rod to strike, but when she looked down at the trembling body, she began to tremble herself and dropped the stick. Stooping down, she raised him up and began kissing him, crying at the same time with tears in her eyes.

'What's going to become of you at all, at all? God save us, I haven't the courage to beat you and you're breaking my heart with your wickedness.'

The boy sobbed, hiding his head in his mother's bosom.

'Go away,' she said, thrusting him away from her, 'and eat your dinner. Your father will give you a good thrashing in the morning. I've spared you often and begged him not to beat you, but this time I'm not going to say a word for you. You've my heart broken, so you have. Come here and eat your dinner.'

She put the dinner on the plate and pushed the boy into the chair. He sat down sobbing, but presently he wiped his eyes with his sleeve and began to eat ravenously. Gradually his face brightened and he moved about on the chair, settling himself more comfortably and forgetting all his fears of his mother and the thrashing he was going to get next morning in the joy of satisfying his hunger. The mother sat on the doorstep, knitting in silence and watching him lovingly from under her long black eyelashes.

All her anger had vanished by now and she felt glad that she had thrust all the responsibility for punishment on to her husband. Still, she wanted to be severe, and although she wanted to ask Stephen what he had been doing, she tried to hold her tongue. At last, however, she had to talk.

'What kept you, Stephen?' she said softly.

Stephen swallowed the last mouthful and turned around with his mug in his hand.

'We were only playing ball,' he said excitedly, 'and then Red Michael ran after us and chased us out of his field where we were playing. And we had to run an awful way; oh, a long, long way we had to run, over crags where I never was before.'

'But didn't I often tell you not to go into people's fields to play ball?'

'Oh, mother, sure it wasn't me but the other boys that wanted to go, and if I didn't go with them they'd say I was afraid, and father says I mustn't be afraid.'

'Yes, you pay heed to your father but you pay no heed to your mother that has all the trouble with you. Now and what would I do if you fell running over the crags and sprained your ankle?'

And she put her apron to her eyes to wipe away a tear.

Stephen left his chair, came over to her and put his arms around her neck.

'Mother,' he said, 'I'll tell you what I saw on the crags if you promise not to tell father about me being late and playing ball in Red Michael's field.'

'I'll do no such thing,' she said.

'Oh, do, mother,' he said, 'and I'll never be late again, never, never, never.'

'All right, Stephen; what did you see, my little treasure?'

He sat down beside her on the threshold and, looking wistfully out into the sky, his eyes became big and dreamy and his face assumed an expression of mystery and wonder.

'I saw a great big black horse,' he said, 'running in the sky over our heads, but none of the other boys saw it but me, and I didn't tell them about it. The horse had seven tails and three heads and its belly was so big you could put our house into it. I saw it with my two eyes. I did, mother. And then it soared and galloped away, away, ever so far. Isn't that a great thing I saw, mother?'

'It is, darling,' she said dreamily, looking out into the sky, thinking of something with soft eyes. There was silence. Then Stephen spoke again without looking at her.

'Sure you won't tell on me, mother?'

'No, treasure, I won't.'

'On your soul you won't?'

'Hush! little one. Listen to the birds. They are beginning to sing. I won't tell at all. Listen to the beautiful ones.'

They both sat in silence, listening and dreaming, both of them.

LIAM O'FLAHERTY

Questions

Why was Brigid Gill alone in her cottage?

What thoughts did she have? (What worries would any parent

have if a child did not come home?)
Why did Brigid get a willow rod?
Why didn't Stephen's mother hit him?
Why was Stephen late?
What did Stephen tell his mother he had seen on the crags?
From the information in the extract, how would you describe
the relationship between Stephen and his mother? Do you like
Stephen? Do you like Stephen's mother?

Discussion
Punishments at home.

Writing
How would you explain Stephen's dream?
'Mother' or 'Father'.

Project
Make a collection of poems and extracts about parents and
children.

Improvisation
Make a play from this extract, and act it in pairs.

'Too late: my father was upon us'

Marcel recalls an event from his childhood. He was about nine years old at the time:

On the evenings when there were visitors, Mamma did not come up to my room. I did not, at that time, have dinner with the family: I came out to the garden after dinner, and at nine I said good night and went to bed. But on these evenings I used to dine earlier than the others, and to come in afterwards and sit at table until eight o'clock, when it was understood that I must go upstairs; that frail and precious kiss which Mamma used always to leave upon my lips when I was in bed and just going to sleep I had to take with me from the dining-room to my own, and to keep all the time that it took me to undress, without letting its sweet charm be broken. . . .

We were all in the garden when the double peal of the gate-bell sounded shyly.

'Ah! There's M. Swann,' cried my father. 'Let's ask him if he thinks it will be fine tomorrow.'

The boy's mother goes to speak to the visitor.

I followed her: I could not bring myself to let her go out of reach of me while I felt that in a few minutes I should have to leave her in the dining-room and go up to my bed without the consoling thought, as on ordinary evenings, that she would come up, later, to kiss me.

But tonight, before the dinner-bell had sounded, my grandfather said with unconscious cruelty: 'The little man looks tired; he'd better go up to bed. Besides, we are dining late tonight.'

And my father, who was less scrupulous than my grandmother or mother in observing the letter of a treaty, went on: 'Yes; run along; to bed with you.'

I would have kissed Mamma then and there, but at that moment the dinner-bell rang.

'No, no, leave your mother alone. You've said good night quite enough. These exhibitions are absurd. Go on upstairs.'

And so I must climb each step of the staircase 'against my heart', as the saying is, climbing in opposition to my heart's desire, which was to return to my mother, since she had not, by her kiss, given my heart leave to accompany me forth.

Once in my room I had to stop every loophole, to close the shutters, to dig my own grave as I turned down the bedclothes, to wrap myself in the shroud of my nightshirt. But before burying myself in the iron bed which had been placed there because, on summer nights, I was too hot among the rep curtains of the four-poster, I was stirred to revolt, and attempted the desperate stratagem of a condemned prisoner. I wrote to my mother begging her to come upstairs for an important reason which I could not put in writing.

But his mother ignores his request; so he decides 'to abandon all attempts to go to sleep without seeing Mamma, and . . . to kiss her at all costs, even with the certainty of being in disgrace with her for long afterwards, when she herself came up to bed'. Finally, he hears the guest leave.

My father and mother were left alone and sat down for a moment; then my father said: 'Well, shall we go up to bed?'

'As you wish, dear, though I don't feel in the least like sleeping. I don't know why; it can't be the coffee-ice – it wasn't strong enough to keep me awake like this.'

My mother opened the latticed door which led from the hall to the staircase. Presently I heard her coming upstairs to close her window. I went quietly into the passage; my heart was beating so violently that I could hardly move, but at least it was throbbing no longer with anxiety, but with terror and with joy. I saw in the well of the stair a light coming upwards, from Mamma's candle. Then I saw Mamma herself: I threw myself upon her. For an instant she looked at me in astonishment, not realizing what could have happened. Then her face assumed an expression of anger. She said not a single word to me; and, for that matter, I used to go for days on end without being spoken to, for far less offences than this.

But she heard my father coming from the dressing-room, where he had gone to take off his clothes, and, to avoid the 'scene' which he would make if he saw me, she said, in a voice half-stifled by her anger: 'Run away at once. Don't let your father see you standing there!'

But I begged her again to 'Come and say good night to me!' terrified as I saw the light from my father's candle already creeping up the wall, but also making use of his approach as a means of blackmail, in the hope that my mother, not wishing him to find me there, as find me he must if she continued to hold out, would give in to me, and say: 'Go back to your room. I will come.'

Too late: my father was upon us. Instinctively I murmured, though no one heard me, 'I am done for!'

I was not, however. He looked at me for a moment with an air of annoyance and surprise, and then when Mamma had told him, not without some embarrassment, what had happened, said to her: 'Go along with him, then; you said just now that you didn't feel like sleep, so stay in his room for a little. I don't need anything.'

'But, dear,' my mother answered timidly, 'whether or not I feel like sleep is not the point; we must not make the child accustomed. . . .'

'There's no question of making him accustomed,' said my father, with a shrug of the shoulders; 'you can see quite well that the child is unhappy. After all, we aren't gaolers. You'll end by making him ill, and a lot of good that will do. There are two beds in his room; stay beside him for the rest of the night. I'm off to bed, anyhow; I'm not nervous like you. Good night.'

It was impossible for me to thank my father. I stood there, not daring to move; he was still confronting us, an immense figure in his white nightshirt, crowned with the pink and violet scarf of Indian cashmere in which, since he had begun to suffer from neuralgia, he used to tie up his head, standing like Abraham telling Sarah that she must tear herself away from Isaac.

Mamma spent that night in my room. . . . My father, as soon as he had grasped the fact that I was unhappy, said to my mother: 'Go and comfort him.'

MARCEL PROUST: *Swann's Way*

Questions
What was the understanding about dinner and bed when there were visitors at the house?
How did the boy's grandfather and father ignore the understanding?
What kind of expressions does the writer use to show how very unhappy he was when he was sent to bed? (Why was his nightshirt a 'shroud'?)

How does the father surprise the boy and his mother?
What do you think of the boy?
What do you think of his mother?
What do you think of his father?

Discussion
How can parents understand better the worries and unhappiness of their children? When should they be firm? When should they be sympathetic?

Writing
A memory of a distressing event which turned out better than you had expected.
'Getting to Bed'.

'Don't tell your mother'

As she grew older, five, six, seven, the connection between her and her father was even stronger.

He was very fond of swimming, and in warm weather would take her down to the canal, to a silent place, or to a big pond or reservoir, to bathe. He would take her on his back as he went swimming, and she clung close, feeling his strong movement under her, so strong, as if it would uphold all the world. Then he taught her to swim.

She was a fearless little thing, when he dared her. And he had a curious craving to frighten her, to see what she would do with him. He said, would she ride on his back whilst he jumped off the canal bridge down into the water beneath.

She would. He mounted the parapet of the canal bridge. The water was a long way down. He leapt, and down they went. The crash of the water as they went under struck through the child's small body. But she remained fixed. And when they came up again, and when they went to the bank, and when they sat on the grass side by side, he laughed, and said it was fine.

When the fair came, she wanted to go in the swingboats. He took her, and, standing up in the boat, holding on to the irons, began to drive higher, perilously higher. The child clung fast on her seat.

'Do you want to go any higher?' he said to her, and she laughed with her mouth, her eyes wide and dilated. They were rushing through the air.

'Yes,' she said, feeling as if she would turn into vapour, lose hold of everything, and melt away. The boat swung far up, then down like a stone, only to be caught sickeningly up again.

'Any higher?' he called, looking at her over his shoulder.

She laughed with white lips.

He sent the swingboat sweeping through the air in a great semicircle, till it jerked and swayed at the high horizontal. The child clung on, pale, her eyes fixed on him. People below were calling. The jerk at the top had almost shaken them both out. He sat down, and let the swing boat swing itself out.

People in the crowd cried shame on him as he came out of the swingboat. He laughed. The child clung to his hand, pale and mute. In a while she was violently sick. He gave her lemonade, and she gulped a little.

'Don't tell your mother you've been sick,' he said.

D. H. LAWRENCE: *The Rainbow*

Questions

. How does the author show that the connection between the father and daughter is growing stronger?

What kind of connection would you say it is?

Why does the father tell his daughter not to tell her mother that she has been sick?

What do you think of the father?

Discussion

How should people be trained or prepared to become good parents?

Writing

A memory of a childhood event involving a relationship with a parent, relative, or adult acquaintance or stranger.

Improvisation

The girl's mother discovers she has been sick. Improvise the scene.

'Tell your mother as 'er mester's
Got hurt i' th' pit—'

Somebody's knockin' at th' door
    Mother, come down an' see!
– I's think it's nobbut a beggar;
    Say I'm busy.

It's not a beggar, mother; hark
    How 'ard 'e knocks!
– Eh, tha'rt a mard-arsed kid,
    'E'll gie thee socks!

Shout an' ax what 'e wants,
    I canna come down.
– 'E says, is it Arthur Holliday's?
    – Say Yes, tha clown.

'E says: Tell your mother as 'er mester's
    Got hurt i' th' pit –
What? Oh my Sirs, 'e never says that,
    That's not it!

Come out o' th' way an' let me see!
    Eh, there's no peace!
An' stop thy scraightin', childt,
    Do shut thy face!

'Your mester's 'ad a accident
    An' they ta'ein' 'im i' th' ambulance
Ter Nottingham.' – Eh dear o' me,
    If 'e's not a man for mischance!

Wheer's 'e hurt this time, lad?
    – I dunna know,
They on'y towd me it wor bad –
    It would be so!

Out o' my way, childt! dear o' me, wheer
    'Ave I put 'is clean stockin's an' shirt?
Goodness knows if they'll be able
    To take off 'is pit-dirt!

An' what a moan 'e'll make! there niver
    Was such a man for a fuss
If anything ailed 'im; at any rate
    I shan't 'ave 'im to nuss.

I do 'ope as it's not so very bad!
    Eh, what a shame it seems
As some should ha'e hardly a smite o' trouble
    An' others 'as reams!

It's a shame as 'e should be knocked about
    Like this, I'm sure it is!
'E's 'ad twenty accidents, if 'e's 'ad one;
    Owt bad, an' it's his!

There's one thing, we s'll 'ave a peaceful 'ouse f'r a bit,
    Thank heaven for a peaceful house!
An' there's compensation, sin' it's accident,
    An' club-money – I won't growse.

An' a fork an' a spoon 'e'll want – an' what else?
    I s'll never catch that train!
What a traipse it is, if a man gets hurt!
    I sh'd think 'e'll get right again.

D. H. LAWRENCE: 'The Collier's Wife'

Questions
How many people speak in this poem?
What does each of them say?
How does the collier's wife take the news?

Write the poem out in your own words as a short play. Act it.

Edvard Munch: Tate Gallery

What does this picture suggest to you? Write a story or description or account of your thoughts or whatever you feel or imagine as you look at it.

Give the picture a title, and describe it as accurately as you can to someone who cannot see it.

'If death should carry me off, do the duties of a father'

Beowulf—6

Beowulf bids Hrothgar goodbye before going to face Grendel's mother.

Beowulf spoke: 'Remember, Hrothgar, now that I am fit for the fray, the bargain we made not long ago – if death should carry me off, you would do the duties of a father. Protect my compatriots, and return to Unferth this ancient heirloom, Hrunting, which will fight for my fame or see death take me.'

After these words Beowulf swiftly set off into the mere without waiting for an answer. The brimming waters closed round the hero. It was the best part of a day before he sighted the bed of the lake.

Straightway she who had dwelt in the deep for half a hundred years, grim, greedy, and hungry, was aware that an adventurer from above was spying on her home. At once she came to grips with him; she fixed Beowulf with her terrible talons, but they could not pierce the ring-mail which so carefully protected his person from the first savage sally of her grasping claws. So the wolfish water woman struggled with him down to the depths and into her own lair, so that he could not make use of his weapons, however brave he might be. Swarms of sea monsters made attacks on him and ripped at his corselet with their terrible tusks.

Then Beowulf discovered that he was in some unaccustomed hostile hall, where he was untroubled by the water which could not encompass him in its eddies, as it was dammed off by a vaulted dome. He saw the flicker of flames, a brilliant light darting brightly.

Our warrior then made out the mighty mere wife, the hag from the hidden depths. He swiftly drove home the battle-sword, crashing resoundingly at her head with the patterned blade. But the intruder discovered that the flashing edge would not bite, and was useless. It was ineffective when its wielder most wanted its power. In times gone by it had done its duty, had often cracked open the helmet and crushed the life out of those destined to die. This was the first time the prized possession failed to live up to its name.

Beowulf, bearing in mind his boast and brave reputation, did not despair, but pitched away the patterned sword and put his trust in his strength of hand. For a hero who wishes to find fame in his exploits must not be too much in love with life. The warrior fixed Grendel's mother by the shoulder, his rage filling him with such strength that he felled her to the floor. She quickly returned the hold and came to grips with him. The strongest of soldiers, weary as he was, faltered and fell. She pounced on her unwelcome guest, and drew her dagger, broad and bright-edged, to avenge her only offspring.

His armoured vest protected his shoulder and preserved his life, against the probing of the piercing knife. Now God took a hand. When Beowulf returned to the attack, the Lord of Right presided.

As Beowulf struggled up he spotted amongst the trappings a trusted battle-blade, an ancient sword forged by the ogres of old, keen along its cutting edge, the pride of former fighters. It was a blade to be envied, but no man of ordinary might could bear it to the battle play, so grand and great it was – the toil of the titans. Berserk and beside himself, well nigh bereft of life, Beowulf heaved up the ring-hilted blade and, raging with the whorled weapon, savagely struck out. The blade bit right through the monster's neck and smashed her spine in pieces. Backwards and forwards the sword slashed her through. She crumpled up on the ground, the sword sweated blood, the hero saw his work was good.

The light leapt up brightly and lit up everything just as heaven's candle in the sky gives bright light. Beowulf scanned the monster's den, and turned along the wall. Angry still and wrathful he held the weapon on high, grasping it firmly by the hilt. The blade was not useless to Beowulf: he intended to use it here and now to extract full vengeance for the many many raids that Grendel had carried out against the Danes – not just the time when he had killed the men in their slumbers, devouring fifteen in their beds and bearing away a booty of fifteen more. Beowulf had settled that account as he now saw full well when he witnessed the corpse of Grendel, dead and destroyed by his battle with Beowulf at Heorot. Though it was lifeless it leapt with the deep lash of the swinging sword stroke, as Beowulf severed the head right from the body.

The band of soldiers who were watching at the water's side with Hrothgar saw the turbulence from the depths and the gore drifting to the surface and staining the mere. The hardened warriors with grey hair spoke together about the hero and agreed that they dare not hope to see Beowulf returning in triumph again to Hrothgar. Most concluded that he had fallen foul of the water hag. The ninth hour of the day arrived. The Spear-Danes left the shore with Hrothgar, the generous donor of gifts. Beowulf's men sat down, sick at heart, and stared at the mere. They hoped against hope to see their friend and leader alive.

Meanwhile the sword blade had begun to dissolve like icicles in the baneful blood. It was a miracle that it all melted like ice when the Father who has sway over wind and water and the changing seasons allows the seas to thaw, and frees all from the fastening frost.

Beowulf took from the many treasures he saw in the sea lair only the head and the precious sword hilt. The blade had melted, the damasked steel already dissolved; so baneful was the acid blood, so venomous that spirit from the other world who had perished there. Soon Beowulf was swimming to the surface, victorious. Now that the fiend's days of life in this transitory world had all been spent, all the waters were purified.

Beowulf swam to the safety of the land, revelling in his trophies from the deep, the great booty he had brought up with him. The bright band of followers went to meet him, thanking God that he had been returned to them safe and sound. Then the hero was quickly helped out of his helmet and corselet. The lake lapped calmly, those waters which the heavens had seen stained by the blood of battle. Then they made their way with happy hearts over the foot-worn ways and paths which now they knew. The brave retainers with difficulty managed to heave Grendel's head along the cliffs. Four of them had their work cut out to ferry it to the gold hall, jammed onto a spear. So at last they arrived at Heorot, fourteen foreigners, bold and warlike, and Beowulf proudly with them, measuring their steps over the meadows to the hall. Beowulf, leader of warriors, bold in bravery, favoured with fortune and high in honour, marched in to greet Hrothgar. Grendel's head was heaved by its hair on to the floor, an eerie vision for the earls with their queen in their midst. It was a fearful and terrifying sight. There the warriors drank, and gazed.

Dictionary or Discussion
   compatriots
   trappings
   titans
   berserk
   whorled
   baneful
   the ninth hour of the day (three o'clock in the afternoon)
   (Can you find out why it was the 'ninth hour'?)

Imagine you are Beowulf, returning safely to your companions. Describe your adventure in the lake.

For discussion. Charms.

Find out about other famous swords in mythology.

To do. Explore part of the countryside which in days of long ago might have been thought to shelter strange creatures. If you like, look up old maps and find out about the old place names and what they mean. Draw a map of the area, and write a story or description of it.
(Near Sittingbourne, in Kent, is a village called Wormshill. The Anglo-Saxon word *wyrm* (worm) meant serpent or dragon. You might like to find out what records exist of strange monsters which *did* live on earth long ago.)

Write or improvise the account which Beowulf gives to Hrothgar of his fight with Grendel's mother. Tell it in the first person.

What do you think are the duties of a father today?
What are the duties of a mother?

Recall the improvisation on page 107. Develop the scene to include Beowulf's journey through the waters to the cave of Grendel's mother.

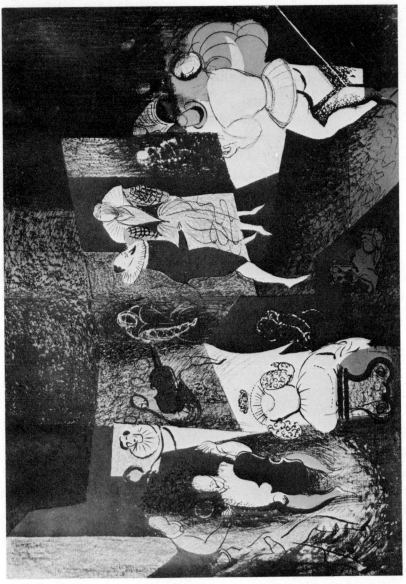

J. Lyons & Co: Apex Photos Ltd.

Picture

What does this picture suggest to you?

(Are the people real? Do you want to give them names? What is the occasion, do you think? Or is it not a real occasion at all? Do you *hear* anything as you look at the picture? Is it serious? Humorous? Frightening? Does the picture give you any special feeling? What title would you suggest for it?)

Although this is a black and white print, this picture was originally in colour. What colours would you give to the picture? Why?

'If you hold the shell to your ear'

Water from the Limpopo

Bottles filled with yellowish water, corked and sealed with sealing wax, stood in rows on the classroom table. They had labels, inscribed in an uneven elderly hand: 'Nile', 'Limpopo', 'Mediterranean'.

There were bottles of water from the Rhine, the Thames, Lake Michigan, from the Dead Sea and the Amazon, but however long we looked at them they all remained equally yellow and uninteresting.

We pestered our geography master Cherpunov to allow us to taste the water from the Dead Sea – we wanted to see if it really was as salty as we were told – but he always refused.

Short, slit-eyed and with a grey beard almost down to his knees, he was nicknamed Merlin.

He was always bringing curious objects with him to illustrate his lessons, but the bottles were his favourites. He told us that he had himself got the water from the Nile in Cairo.

'Just look,' he would shake the bottle, 'look at all that sediment. Nile water is richer than gold. The culture of Ancient Egypt was based on mud. Markovsky, tell the class what is meant by culture.'

Markovsky stood up and said culture was the cultivation of wheat, raisins and rice.

'An idiotic answer, but there's something in it,' commented Cherpunov, turning to his other bottles.

He was very proud of the one from the Limpopo, which had been sent to him as a present by a former pupil.

Cherpunov devised his own visual aids to geography. He would draw three *A*'s on the blackboard, one inside the other, put a *B* inside the smallest *A* and say:

'Now remember, the big *A* stands for Asia, Arabia is in Asia, Aden is in Arabia and the British are in Aden.'

We immediately memorized this for life.

The seniors told us that Cherpunov had arranged a small geographical museum in his flat but would allow no one to see it. It was said to include a stuffed humming-bird, a collection of butterflies, a telescope, and even a nugget of gold.

These stories inspired me to start a collection of my own. It was, of course, a modest one, but in my imagination it was priceless, unique. Each object, whether a dead praying mantis or a button off a Rumanian soldier's uniform, had a colourful legend attached to it.

One day I came across Cherpunov sitting on a bench in the Botanical Gardens. The bench was still wet from the rain. He was poking the ground with his stick.

I took off my cap and bowed.

'Hallo,' he said, holding out his hand. 'Come and sit down. I hear you're making a collection. What have you got in it?'

I shyly gave him the list of my simple treasures. He grinned.

'Most commendable. Come and see me on Sunday morning. I'll show you mine. Perhaps one day you'll be a geographer or an explorer – as you seem to be so interested in these things.'

'With my mother?' I asked.

'What about your mother?'

'Shall I come with my mother?'

'No – why? – come by yourself. Mothers don't understand about geography.'

Next Sunday I put on my uniform and went to call on Cherpunov. He lived in a small cottage in the suburb of Pechersk. Lilac bushes grew so thickly round it that they made it dark inside.

It was a day in late autumn. The lilac bushes, still green, stood dripping in the mist. Steamers hooted on the Dnieper at the foot of the hill, saying goodbye to Kiev and going off to their winter quarters.

I climbed the front steps, pulled the brass handle of the old-fashioned bell and heard it tinkle inside.

Cherpunov, in a warm grey jacket and felt shoes, opened the door.

The house was filled with marvels.

Standing in the hall, I saw in an oval mirror the reflection of a small boy, red with embarrassment, struggling with stiff fingers to undo the buttons of his greatcoat – I didn't at once realize it was myself. As I persevered with the buttons, I looked at the frame. It was a wreath of pale glass flowers, leaves and bunches of grapes.

'That's Venetian glass,' said Cherpunov, helping me with the buttons and hanging up my coat. 'Have a good look at it. Touch it if you like.'

I cautiously touched a glass rose. It was almost opaque, as if dusted with powder, but a shaft of light from the next room shone through it with a crimson glow.

'It's like Turkish Delight!'

'Idiotic, but there's something in it,' muttered Cherpunov.

I blushed so that my eyes smarted. He patted my shoulder.

'Sorry, that's only a saying I have. Well, come along. You'll have tea with us.'

I started to say no, but he took me by the elbow and led me into the dining-room. It was less a room than a garden. To reach my place, I had to shift the leaves of a philodendron plant and some long branches dangling from the ceiling, with aromatic red cones on them. Palm leaves fanned out on the table. Vases of pink, yellow and white flowers crowded the window-sills.

I sat down, but immediately jumped up again as a slight young woman with shining grey eyes came rustling swiftly into the room.

'That's the boy I told you about, Masha,' said Cherpunov, 'the son of Georgy Maximovich.'

The girl held out her hand. A bracelet tinkled on her wrist.

'Are you really going to show him everything, Pyotr Petrovich?' she asked him, glancing at me with an amused smile.

'Yes, as soon as we've had tea.'

'Then I'll take a walk into town while you are doing it. I want to get a cake at Kircheim's, and one or two other things.'

'As you wish.'

She poured out tea with lemon and put a plate of Vienna rolls in front of me.

'You'd better tuck in. You'll need your strength.'

After tea Cherpunov lit a cigarette. He flicked the ash into a seashell edged with the palest of pink petrified foam. There were two of them on the table. 'These come from New Guinea,' he told me.

'Well, goodbye,' said the girl in a loud voice, getting up and going from the room. . . .

The girl came back and stood in the doorway. She had a small black hat on her head and was pulling on her left glove.

'Incidentally, what is poetry?' Cherpunov suddenly asked me. 'No, I don't expect you to answer. You can't define it, anyway. But take this shell. It comes from Maklaï's island. If you look at it long enough, it suddenly occurs to you that there was once a morning when the sunshine fell on it in such a way that it will stay on it for ever.'

The girl sat down and began to take off her glove.

I was staring at the shell. For a moment I really thought I had dropped off to sleep and was seeing a slow dawn and the pink flash of the sunrise over the translucent waste of ocean waters.

'If you hold the shell to your ear,' Cherpunov's voice came from a long way off, 'you can hear a rumbling – I can't tell you why. No one can tell you. It's a mystery. Anything the human mind is incapable of grasping is a mystery.'

The girl took off her hat and put it on her lap.

'Try it,' said Cherpunov.

I pressed the shell to my ear and heard a sleepy murmur, as of surf breaking on a very distant shore. The girl held out her hand:

'Let me try. It's a long time since I've listened to it.'

I gave her the shell. She held it to her ear and smiled, half opening her lips and showing small and very white, moist teeth.

'Aren't you going to Kircheim's, Masha?' Cherpunov asked.

'I've changed my mind. It bores me to go to Kircheim's by myself. I'm sorry if I disturbed you.'

She left the dining-room.

'Well then, let's go on with our conversation, young man,' said Cherpunov. 'You see those black boxes, over in the corner. Bring me the top one, will you. Only be careful how you carry it.'

I picked it up and put it on the table in front of him. It turned out to be quite light.

Cherpunov raised the lid with deliberation. I looked over his shoulder and gasped. Lying on the black silk lining of the box was an enormous black butterfly; it was larger than a maple leaf and it shimmered like a rainbow.

'That's not how you must look at it,' Cherpunov said crossly. 'Look at it this way.'

He took hold of my head and turned it, now to the right, now to the left. The wings of the butterfly flashed white, gold, crimson and blue, as if it were blazing in a magic fire which burned without ever consuming it.

'It's an extremely rare butterfly from the island of Borneo,' Cherpunov said proudly, shutting the lid.

After that he showed me an astral globe, some old maps with the sign of the four Winds on them, and several stuffed humming-birds with beaks as long as bradawls.

'Well, that's enough for today,' he said finally. 'You're tired. Come again any Sunday you like.'

'Are you always at home?'

'Yes. I'm too old now to go wandering about the world, so I do my travelling in my room.' He nodded at the bookshelves and the dead humming-birds.

I was struggling into the sleeves of my coat when the girl came into the hall. She had put on a short, close-fitting jacket, and her hat and gloves. A short dark veil, lowered over her eyes, made them seem quite blue.

We went off together. Cherpunov stood watching us from the door.

'Do be careful, Masha, I beg of you,' he called after her. 'And don't be away too long.'

'All right,' she said without turning round.

We passed the Nikolsky Fort with its bronze lion heads over the gateway, walked across Marinsky Park and turned into Institute Street. The girl was silent. So was I. I was afraid of her asking me some question I would have to answer.

'What did you like best in the collection?' she asked finally.

'The butterfly,' I said after some thought. 'Only I'm sorry for it.'

'Really? Why?'

'Well, it's so beautiful and practically no one ever sees it.'

'What else did you like?'

In the Kreshchatik she stopped outside Kircheim's and asked me if I was allowed to go into pastry shops to have cocoa and cakes. I didn't know if I was or not, but I remembered that I had once been to Kircheim's with Mama and Galya and that we had in fact had cocoa, so I said I was certainly allowed to go to Kircheim's.

'Good. Let's go.'

We sat at a table at the back of the shop. The girl moved a vase of hydrangeas out of the way and ordered two cups of cocoa and a fruit tart.

'Which form are you in at school?'

'The second.'

'And how old are you?'

'Twelve.'

'I'm twenty-eight. When you are twelve, of course, you can believe anything.'

'What do you mean?'

'Do you invent games, and tell yourself stories?'

'Yes.'

'So does Pyotr Petrovich. I don't, it's a pity. I wish you'd put me into yours. We could play together.'

'Play at what?' I asked, getting interested.

'I don't know. Cinderella perhaps. Or at running away from a sorcerer. Or we might invent a new game and call it the Butterfly from the Isle of Borneo.'

'Good,' I said, my imagination taking fire. 'We'll go to a magic forest and look for a well of living water.'

'At the risk of our lives, of course.'

'Of course.'

'We'll bring the water away in our cupped hands,' she said, raising her veil. 'And when one of us gets tired, the other will take over, only we'll have to be very careful not to spill the water as we make the change.'

'But a few drops will get spilled all the same. And where they fall. . . .'

'Big bushes of white flowers will spring up!' she interrupted. 'And what do we do next?'

'We sprinkle the butterfly with the water and it comes to life.'

'And turns into a lovely maiden,' she laughed. 'Well, it's time to go. I expect they're waiting for you at home.'

She came with me as far as Fundukleyev Street and there we parted. I looked back and saw her crossing the Kreshchatik. She looked back at the same moment, and smiled and waved her small gloved hand.

At home, I told no one about having been to Kircheim's, not even Mama who wanted to know why I wasn't eating my dinner. Obstinately silent, I kept thinking about the girl who puzzled me completely.

Next day I asked one of the seniors who the girl was.

'Are you actually telling me you've been to Cherpunov's flat?'

'Yes.'

'And you saw his collection?'

'Yes.'

'Wonders will never cease! The girl is his wife. She's thirty-five years younger than he is.'

I didn't go to see Cherpunov next Sunday because he was ill and had stayed away from school since the middle of the week. A few days later, as we were having tea in the evening, Mama asked me whether I had met a young woman at Cherpunov's.

I said I had and blushed.

'Can it be true?' said Mama, looking at my father. 'They say he was so good to her. She was like a princess in a golden cage.'

Papa said nothing.

'You've had your tea, Kostik,' said Mama. 'Go to your room. It's nearly your bedtime.'

I refrained from listening at the door, although I longed to know what had happened to Cherpunov.

I heard all about it at school. His wife had left him and gone off to Petersburg. The old man was breaking his heart and refusing to see anyone.

'Serves Merlin right,' said my classmate Littauer. 'Never marry a young wife.'

We were fond of old Cherpunov, and very indignant at Littauer. . . .

Cherpunov never appeared at the school again. He had given up his job.

A year later I met him in the street. His face puffy and yellow, he was dragging himself along with difficulty, leaning on his stick. He stopped me, asked me how I was getting on with my work, and said:

'You remember my butterfly from Borneo? I haven't got it any more.'

I said nothing. He looked at me searchingly.

'I gave it to the University. I gave away all my collection of butterflies. Well, goodbye, keep well. I'm glad we met.'

He died shortly afterwards. I remembered Cherpunov and the girl for a long time. An obscure anxiety came over me whenever I thought of her bracelet, and of the way she smiled and waved to me as she crossed the Kreshchatik.

Years later when I was in my top form at school, our teacher of psychology, as he was talking about the creative power of the imagination, suddenly asked us:

'Do you remember Cherpunov?'

'Yes, of course.'

'Well, I can tell you now that there was never anything in his bottles except ordinary water from the tap. You'll ask me why he lied to you. He rightly believed that he was stimulating your imagination. He attached great value to it. I remember him telling me that it was all that distinguished man from the beasts. It was imagination, he said, that had created art, it expanded the boundaries of the world and of the mind, and communicated the quality we call poetry to our lives.'

KONSTANTIN PAUSTOVSKY: *Story of a Life*

Questions
What do you think of Cherpunov? (Do you think, on the evidence here, that he was a good teacher?)
What do you think of Masha?

Writing
Imagine you are a pupil of Cherpunov. Write a letter about Cherpunov to someone you know well.
Make up a story, and put Masha in it.

Discussion
'When you are twelve you can believe anything.'

Game
Invent a game called 'The Butterfly from the Isle of Borneo'.

Improvisation
Turn the story Masha and Kostik begin to invent into several
scenes of a play. Add ideas of your own.

Project
Invent some visual aids which you think would be a help in
teaching your colleagues or the pupils in another form.

Pictures
Give one overall title to these three pictures, and then give each
of the pictures an individual caption.
Write a poem, or an account of your thoughts or feelings as you
look at the pictures.
Tell a story called 'April Fool!' (If you like, you can tell it from
the point of view of the animal(s) or man you see in the pictures.)
Write a commentary for a television or radio programme
entitled 'The Big Fight'.

Alan Root

171

'What shall I do? Where shall I go?'

Mouche, an orphan girl in Paris, is unable to get work and has no one to turn to:

In Paris, in the spring of our times, a young girl was about to throw herself into the Seine.

She was a thin awkward creature with a wide mouth and short black hair. Her body was all bones and hollows where there should have been curves and flesh. Her face was appealing, but it was now gaunt with hunger and the misery of failure. Her eyes were haunting, large, liquid, dark, and filled with despair.

As she is on her way to the river, she passes a puppet show, and the puppets talk to her.

. . . there appeared then finally one more puppet, an old gentleman who wore square steel-rimmed spectacles, a stocking cap, and leather apron. The expression painted on his face contrived sometimes to be quizzical and friendly, at others, when he moved his head, searching and benign. For a moment he appeared to look right through Mouche.

Then in a gentle voice he spoke to her saying, 'Good evening to you. My name is Monsieur Nicholas. I am a maker and mender of toys. My child, I can see you are in trouble. Behind your eyes are many more tears that you have shed.'

Mouche's hand flew to her throat because of the ache that had come to lodge there. It had been so long since anyone had called her 'child'.

Monsieur Nicholas said, 'Perhaps you would care to tell me about it.'

Golo appeared again. He said, 'You tell *him*, Miss. He is a good man. Everybody who has troubles tells them to Monsieur Nicholas.'

Now the tears came swiftly to Mouche's eyes and with their flow something loosened inside her so that standing there in the garish light before the shabby puppet booth and the single animated wooden doll listening so attentively to her, the story of her trials and failures poured from her in moving innocence, for she could not have confessed it thus to any human.

When she had reached the end of her unhappy tale, Monsieur

172

Nicholas concluded for her, '. . . and so you were going to throw yourself in the Seine tonight.'

Mouche stared, marvelling. 'How did you know?'

'It was not hard to tell. There is nothing to seek for one as young as you at the bottom of the river.'

'But, Monsieur Nicholas – what shall I do? Where shall I go?'

The puppet bowed his head as he reflected gravely for a moment, a tiny hand held to his brow. Then he tilted his head to one side and asked, 'Would you care to come with us?'

'Come with you? Oh, could I? Do you suppose I could?' It was as though suddenly a vista of Heaven had opened for Mouche. For she loved them already, all of these queer, compelling little individuals who each in a few brief moments had captured her imagination or tugged at her heartstrings. To make-believe for ever – or as the day was long, to escape from reality into this unique world of fantasy. . . . She held out her arms in supplication and cried, 'Oh, Monsieur Nicholas! Would you really take me with you?'

The puppet contemplated silently for a moment and then said, 'You must ask Poil du Carot. Officially, he manages the show. Good-bye.'

The stage remained empty for an appreciable time. Then an insouciant[1] whistling was heard and Poil du Carot appeared bouncing jauntily along the counter, looking nowhere in particular. As though surprised he said, 'Oh, hello, Mouche, you still here?'

The girl was uncertain how to approach him. He was mercurial.[2] His mood now seemed to be quite different. She ventured, 'Monsieur Nicholas said. . . .'

Carrot Top nodded. 'Oh yes. I heard about it.'

'May I come please, dear Carrot Top?'

The doll with the worried expression looked her over.

'When you ask so prettily it is hard to refuse. . . . After all, it was I who discovered you, wasn't it? However, if you come with us you wouldn't always be telling me what to do, would you? You know I have a lot of responsibility with this show.'

'Oh no. . . .'

'But you'd look after us, wouldn't you?'

'If you'd let me. . . .'

[1] *insouciant:* carefree
[2] *mercurial:* changeable

'Sew on buttons and things?'

'Darn socks. . . .'

'We have no feet,' Carrot Top said severely. 'That's the first thing you'll have to learn.'

'Then I'd knit you mittens.'

Carrot Top nodded. 'That would be nice. We've never had mittens. There'd be no money, you know. . . .'

'I wouldn't care. . . .'

'Very well then. . . . In that case you can come. . . .'

'Oh, Carrot Top!'

'Mouche!'

Mouche never knew exactly how it happened, but suddenly she was close to the booth, weeping with joy, and Carrot Top had both his arms around her neck and was patting her cheek with one of his little wooden hands. He wailed, 'Mouche, don't cry. I always meant you to come. I only had to pretend because I'm the manager. . . . Welcome to Poil du Carot and the family of Capitaine Coq.'

From below there sounded the sardonic yapping of the fox and the shrill voice of Gigi, 'Why does she have to come with us? There isn't enough for everybody now.' Madame Muscat whisked across the stage once croaking, 'Remember, I warned you.' Ali arose and rumbled: 'Gee, I'm glad. I need looking after because I'm so stupid. Scratch my head. . . .'

Carrot Top suddenly became efficient, 'Not now, Ali. We've got to get cracking. Golo . . . Golo, where are you?'

'Right here, little boss.' The Senegalese appeared from behind the booth.

'Mouche is coming with us. Find her a place in the car. . . .'

The negro shouted, 'Bravo. That's mighty good luck for us. I find her a place in the car.'

'Then come back and strike[1] the set, Golo.'

'Yes, sir, little boss. Strike the set. I'll do that. You come along with me, Miss, and I fix you right up.' He picked up Mouche's valise and went with her to the Citroen where he stowed it in the luggage boot in the rear. Then he looked into the back seat of the car which was buried beneath pieces of old clothing, newspapers, maps, bits of costumes for the puppets, and props, packages, a bottle of beer, a half-eaten loaf of bread, tools, and a spare tin of petrol along with other masculine litter.

[1] *strike:* take down, remove

Golo began a futile rummaging. 'Don't look like they's much room, but. . . .'

Mouche took over. 'Never mind, Golo. I promised Carrot Top I'd look after things. I'll have it tidied up in no time.'

As she worked, Mouche sang, '*Va t'en,*[1] *va t'en, va t'en . . .*', humming the melody happily to herself. But through her head were running new words to the old song. 'Go away, death! You are not my lover any longer. I have found a new one called life. It is to him I shall always be faithful. . . .'

She cleared a small space for herself on the seat, folded the clothing and the maps, wrapped the bread and a piece of sausage she found, stowed the costumes carefully where they would not get dirty, and while she was at it, gave a good brushing and cleaning to the old car which in a sense was to be her future home, one that she would share with Carrot Top, Reynardo, Ali, Madame Muscat and Gigi, Golo, and all the rest.

So bemused and enchanted was she that not once did she give a thought to that other who would also be there, the unseen puppeteer who animated the seven dolls.

PAUL GALLICO: *The Love of Seven Dolls*

Questions

How is it that Monsieur Nicholas guesses that Mouche is in trouble?

What is Carrot Top's job?

What conditions does he make if Mouche wants to go with the show?

To whom does Mouche not give a thought?

Discussion

Why do people become miserable? What is the best way to help them?

Writing

Describe Mouche's eventual meeting with the puppeteer, as you imagine it. (What is the puppeteer like?)

Invent a later episode in Mouche's adventures with the show.

Drama

Make a set of puppets, full size if possible, of the characters in this story.

Rewrite the story as a play for the puppets you have made.

[1] *Va t'en:* Go away

G. Rouault: © S.P.A.D.E.M., Paris 1971

What does this face suggest to you? Describe the expression and features as accurately as you can to someone who cannot see the picture. Write a story involving this character. Bring yourself into the story if you wish.

The School You Would Like?

I think it would be a very good idea to have less corporal punishment – as some of the methods these days are appalling, for instance when a teacher hits you with the strap it makes you mutter at them and it also makes you despise them all the more. I don't see no reason for it.

FRANCES, 12

'Clouds now melt like mercy into tears'

Description of a Thunderstorm

Slow boiling up, on the horizon's brim,
Huge clouds arise, mountainous, dark and grim,
Sluggish and slow upon the air they ride,
As pitch-black ships o'er the blue ocean glide;
Curling and hovering o'er the gloomy south,
As curls the sulphur from the cannon's mouth.
More grisly in the sun the tempest comes,
And through the wood with threatened vengeance hums,
Hissing more loud and loud among the trees:
The frightened wild-wind trembles to a breeze,
Just turns the leaf in terrifying sighs,
Bows to the spirit of the storm, and dies.
In wild pulsations beats the heart of fear,
At the low rumbling thunder creeping near,
Like as I've heard the river's flood, confined
Thro' the gulled locks, hangs grumbling on the wind.
The poplar leaf now resteth on its tree;
And the mill-sail, once twirling rapidly,
Lagging and lagging till breeze had dropt,
Abruptly now in hesitation stopt.
The very cattle gaze upon the gloom,
And seemly dread the threatened fate to come.
The little birds sit mute within the bush,
And nature's very breath is stopt and hush.
The shepherd leaves his unprotected flock,
And flies for shelter in some scooping rock;
There hides in fear from the dread boding wrath,
Lest rocks should tremble when it sallies forth,
And that Almighty Power, that bids it roar,
Hath seal'd the doom when time shall be no more.
The cotter's family cringe round the hearth,
Where all is sadden'd but the cricket's mirth;
The boys through fear in soot-black corner push,
And 'tween their father's knees for safety crush;
Each leaves his plaything on the brick-barr' floor,

The idle top and ball can please no more,
And oft above the wheel's unceasing thrum
The murmur's heard to whisper – 'Is it come?'
The clouds more dismal darken on the eye,
More huge, more fearful, and of deeper dye;
And, as unable to light up the gloom,
The sun drops sinking in its bulging tomb.
Now as one glizes skyward with affright,
Short vivid lightnings catch upon the sight;
While like to rumbling armies, as it were,
Th' approaching thunder mutters on the ear,
And still keeps creeping on more loud and loud,
And stronger lightnings splinter through the cloud.
An awe-struck monument of hope and fear,
Mute expectation waits the terror near,
That dreadful clap, that terminates suspense,
When ruin meets us or is banish'd hence.
The signal's giv'n in that explosive flash –
One moment's pause amid the clouds hell-black,
And then the red fire-bolt and horrid crash:
Almighty, what a shock! – the jostled wrack
Of nature seems in mingled ruins done;
Astounded echo rives the terrors back,
And tingles on the ear a dying swoon.
Flash, peal, and flash still rend the melting cloud;
All nature seems to sign her race is o'er,
And as she shrinks 'neath chaos' dismal shroud,
Gives meek consent that suns shall shine no more.
Where is the sinner now, with careless eye,
Will look, and say that all is chance's whim;
When hell e'en trembles at God's majesty,
And sullen owns that naught can equal Him?
But clouds now melt like mercy into tears,
And nature's Lord His wrath in kindness stops:
Each trembling cotter now delighted hears
The rain fall down in heavy-pattering drops.
The sun 'gins tremble through the cloud again,
And a slow murmur wakes the delug'd plain;
A number of thanksgiving, mix'd with fear,
For God's great power and our deliverance here.

JOHN CLARE

179

Questions
From the description in the poem, what signs would suggest to you that a thunderstorm was on its way?
How is the suspense built up? How is it released?

Dictionary or Discussion
   gulled locks
   cotter
   thrum
   glizes
   whim

Writing
'A Hymn to Protect Us against Storms.'
'A Prayer of Thanksgiving for Deliverance from the Storm.'

Music
Beethoven's Sixth Symphony (the 'Pastoral'); *The Thunder and Lightning Polka* by Strauss; *Night on the Bare Mountain* by Mussorgsky (arranged Rimsky-Korsakov).

'So long as I rule these wide realms gifts will be exchanged'

Beowulf—7

Beowulf spoke: 'Behold! the sea-spoils which you gaze on we have brought as signs of our success. I would not have escaped had not God protected me. But I promise you that you can at last sleep easy in your beds, without dread of death from those depths which have filled you with fear in the past.'

Then the golden hilt of the sword from the lake was given to Hrothgar. He looked closely at the legend inscribed on the hilt of the ancient heirloom. It depicted the destruction of the giants of old by the deluge of flooding waters. On the bright golden guard magical runic signs revealed who was the original owner of the sword with twisted hilt and serpent patternings.

Hrothgar spoke: 'Beowulf, my friend, you are famous far and near! You wear your prowess in war wisely and modestly. It sometimes happens that when men are granted good fortune they become too proud. They forget their duty and fail in their generosity. When death overtakes such a one, another is ready to take his place and be generous with all the wealth the other had hoarded.

'Watch out for such a fall, famous friend! Beware pride, like the plague! Now, for a while, is the glory of strength yours; but by and by either sickness or the sword will sap your strength, or consuming fire, or force of flood, or stab of steel or flight of arrow, or hideous old age. Or the brightness of your eyes will fade and darken, and at the last death will defeat you, brave warrior!

'Go now with this advice, take your place and enjoy the banquet to the full. When the morning comes we shall share a host of treasures!' Then they banqueted as was fitting, until the time came for them to take their rest. Soon Beowulf, weary with his adventure, was fast asleep under a great golden roof. He slept until the black raven brightly proclaimed the start of another day.

Now bright light sent the shadows fleeing. The warriors made haste. They were ready and eager for home, and Beowulf wished to rejoin his distant ship. He returned Hrunting to Unferth, too courteous to complain of its cutting edge. When all was ready,

Beowulf addressed Hrothgar: 'Now it is time for us to seek our distant homes over the sea. You have hosted us handsomely. I shall always be at your service. If ever I hear you are in need of me, I shall return with a thousand men to your aid.'

Hrothgar replied: 'Never have I heard a young man speak as you do. If it should happen that spear or grim battle, disease or the sword should kill your prince Hygelac while you keep your life, then I can think of no better successor as king and protector of his precious wealth than yourself, if you should so wish to rule the land of your forefathers. The better I know you, the more I admire you, my dear Beowulf.

'You have sealed a firm friendship between our two peoples. So long as I rule these wide realms gifts will be exchanged. Many a man will greet his companion with good things over the waters where the gannets bathe; and ships with curved prows will bring presents and friendly offerings over the ocean. I know your people are reliable in war and peace, because they hold fast to the old and honourable ways.'

Then Hrothgar gave to Beowulf in the hall twelve treasures, bade him take them with good health back to his own people, and come again before too long. Tears pouring down his aged face, grey-haired Hrothgar embraced and kissed Beowulf. He knew the chances were that they would never meet again in this world. He had taken to Beowulf so much that he could not hide his heartbreak. Deep within him, a secret sadness consumed him, so dear was his love for the young hero.

Then Beowulf, loaded with gold and delighted with his treasures, took the green ways back to where his ship was awaiting him. On their way they sang the praises of Hrothgar's generosity. He was a king beyond reproach, until the bane of old age deprived him of the joys of strength.

Dictionary or Discussion
  legend
  runic
  consuming

Imagine that you are Beowulf, safely bound for home after this adventure. You send messages ahead to King Hygelac, giving your impression of Hrothgar, and mentioning the advice Hrothgar has given you. Write the message you might send.

For discussion. The pleasures and pains of old age.

Find out what you can about runes, and also about the Franks'
Casket.

To do. Investigate ancient accounts of floods (e.g. Noah's flood).

Invent and describe in detail one of the twelve treasures Hrothgar
might have given to Beowulf.

Make up a ballad about Hrothgar's generosity.

An exact or literal translation of some of the Anglo-Saxon poetry
in Beowulf would give expressions such as:
creatures from elsewhere
yellow like an apple
swan's riding place
bath of the gannets
the world candle
bone-chamber
treasure-giver
with mixed hair
dweller upon earth
whale's riding place
battle-pole

Suggest more colloquial or everyday ways of rendering these
expressions into modern English (e.g. sea-garment – which en-
wraps the mast – might be simply rendered as 'sail').

II (4) **Of homecomings**

1. *'Billy! Billy, come back here!'*
2. *'Thy brother is come'*
3. *'Your brother has come home'*
4. *'I thank God that you are home safe and sound'*

'Billy! Billy, come back here!'

Billy is supposed to have made a bet on some horses for his elder brother, Jud. Instead of giving the money to the bookmaker for the bet, Billy keeps it, thinking that his brother will never know if the horses do not win – because Jud would lose his money anyway. But the horses do win, and when Jud goes to collect the ten pounds he thinks he has won he discovers that Billy has not placed the bet. In revenge, Jud kills the hawk Billy has trained and loved.

'Where is it, Jud? What you done wi' it?'

He turned away to the fireplace and replaced the poker flat in the hearth.

'It's in t'bin.'

Billy broke from between them, out through the kitchen to the dustbin at the side of the garage. He yanked the lid off and peered down. It was black inside so he reached down, fingers feeling lightly amongst the rubbish. Then he stopped feeling, and straightened up quickly, holding the hawk in his hand.

He carried it into the kitchen and stood with his back to the living-room door to inspect it. Brown eyes open. Glass eyes. Curved beak ajar, tongue just visible in the slit. Head lolling downwards, swinging whichever way he turned it to brush away the dust and ashes from the feathers. Blowing the feathers clean, raising them with his breath, then smoothing them gently into place with his fingers.

He opened one wing like a fan, and on the underside of it slowly drew a finger down the primaries, down to the body, as though the wing was a feathered instrument, its note too soft for human hearing. He refolded the wing carefully across its back, then carried it through to the living-room.

Jud was standing with his back to the fire. His mother was standing at the table, pouring tea. The comic was still on the floor.

'Look what he's done, mam! Look at it!'

He held the hawk out to her across the table, yellow legs upwards, jesses dangling, its claws hooks in the air.

'I know, it's a shame, love; but I don't want it.'

187

She sat down, bringing her face on a level with the hawk.

'Look at it, though! Look what he's done!'

She looked at it, curling her top lip, then turned to Jud.

'It wa' a rotten trick, Jud.'

'It wa' a rotten trick what he did, wasn't it?'

'I know, but you know how much he thought about that bird.'

'He didn't think half as much about it as I did about that ten quid.'

'He thought world on it though. Take it away from t'table then, Billy.'

'It wasn't worth ten quid was it?'

'I know, but it wa' a rotten trick all t'same. Take it away from my face then, Billy, I've seen it.'

Billy tried to get close to her with the bird, but she wouldn't let him.

'It's not fair on him, mam! It's not fair.'

'I know it's not, but it's done now so there's nowt we can do about it, is there?'

'What about him though? What you goin' to do to him? I want you to do summat to him.'

'What can I do?'

'Hit him! Gi' him a good hiding! Gi' him some fist!'

Jud snorted and turned round to look at himself in the mirror above the mantelpiece.

'I'd like to see her.'

'Talk sense, Billy, how can I hit him?'

'You never do owt to him! He gets away wi' everything!'

'O! Shut up now then! You've cried long enough about it.'

'You're not bothered about owt, you.'

'Course I'm bothered. But it's only a bird. You can get another, can't you?'

She looked down at her magazine and raised her cup. Billy clenched his free hand and swung at it, fisting it clear off its handle across the room, shooting out a tongue of tea. Jud, watching the scene through the mirror, was too slow to interpret the reverse order of events, and before he had time to turn or step aside both cup and tea hit him smack between the shoulder-blades. Mrs Casper was left looking at the lug crooked on her finger. Billy followed the tea and the cup on to Jud's back, grasping him round the neck with both arms. Jud swung him round like a maypole hanger. Mrs Casper jumped up and tried to drag him off. He kicked out at her like a hare, and she doubled up back into the table holding her breasts. The pot wobbled. The packet of biscuits and the milk bottle fell over. The bottle rolled off the table and smashed. The biscuits were stopped by the swamp of milk on the cloth.

Billy was screaming and crying into Jud's ears. Jud was trying to reach over and grasp him by the hair, but every time his hand came back Billy swayed backwards or sideways out of its reach. Then, with a quick duck, Jud flicked him over his head. Billy kept hold until the impetus of his somersaulting body made him let go, and he swung over to land knees and chest against the back of the settee, knocking it over, making the front castors squeal and spin, and revealing the pouched hessian bottom. They both went for him. Billy stood up, and, holding the hawk by the feet, swung it at them. Its wings opened, and the open eyes and the rush of feathers before their faces halted them long enough for Billy to hurdle the upturned settee and dart out between them, banging both doors behind him.

As he ran up the path to the front gate, neighbours clustered at half-open doors, and at their own front gates to watch him. He jumped up on the wall, down to the pavement and bent down at the gutter, feeling in the running water for a stone or a pebble.

'Billy! Billy, come back here!'

He turned at the voice. His mother was run-walking up the path, glancing around at all the neighbours as she came. She reached the gate, but before she had time to open it, Billy was away, up the avenue. She stood gripping the pointed verticals, watching him into the distance.

BARRY HINES: *A Kestrel for a Knave*

Questions
What did Billy's mother think of Jud's treatment of the bird?
How did Jud defend his action?
What did Billy want his mother to do about it?
What do you think of Billy's mother?

Imagine that Billy and Jud have to present their cases before an impartial judge. They are allowed to have one friend each to speak on their behalf. Write or improvise:

(*a*) the speech Billy's friend might make, defending Billy and attacking Jud;

(*b*) the speech Jud's friend might make, defending Jud and attacking Billy;

(*c*) the judge's verdict.

Discussion

Are people too sentimental about animals?

Project

Find out about betting and the law. What are betting shops? Who wins? Who loses? Is betting a good or bad thing? What is the attitude of 'the State' towards betting? What seem to be the pleasures of betting? What seem to be the pains? Is betting on horses worse than doing football pools, or buying premium bonds, or a raffle ticket at a church fête? Why do people bet? What is the church attitude towards it?

Find out what dangers to health pets may bring.

The prodigal son's homecoming (*1*)

11 And he said, A certain man had two sons:

12 And the younger of them said to *his* father, Father, give me the portion of goods that falleth *to me*. And he divided unto them *his* living.

13 And not many days after the younger son gathered all together, and took his journey into a far country, and there wasted his substance with riotous living.

14 And when he had spent all, there arose a mighty famine in that land; and he began to be in want.

15 And he went and joined himself to a citizen of that country; and he sent him into his fields to feed swine.

16 And he would fain have filled his belly with the husks that the swine did eat; and no man gave unto him.

17 And when he came to himself, he said, How many hired servants of my father's have bread enough and to spare, and I perish with hunger!

18 I will arise and go to my father, and will say unto him, Father, I have sinned against heaven and before thee,

19 And am no more worthy to be called thy son: make me as one of thy hired servants.

20 And he arose, and came to his father. But when he was yet a great way off, his father saw him, and had compassion, and ran, and fell on his neck, and kissed him.

21 And the son said unto him, Father, I have sinned against heaven, and in thy sight, and am no more worthy to be called thy son.

22 But the father said to his servants, Bring forth the best robe, and put *it* on him, and put a ring on his hand, and shoes on *his* feet:

23 And bring hither the fatted calf, and kill *it*; and let us eat, and be merry:

24 For this my son was dead, and is alive again; he was lost, and is found. And they began to be merry.

25 Now his elder son was in the field: and as he came and drew nigh to the house, he heard musick and dancing.

26 And he called one of the servants, and asked what these things meant.

27 And he said unto him, Thy brother is come; and thy father hath killed the fatted calf, because he hath received him safe and sound.

28 And he was angry, and would not go in; therefore came his father out, and intreated him.

29 And he answering said to *his* father, Lo, these many years do I serve thee, neither transgressed I at any time thy commandment: and yet thou never gavest me a kid, that I might make merry with my friends:

30 But as soon as this thy son was come, which hath devoured thy living with harlots, thou hast killed for him the fatted calf.

31 And he said unto him, Son, thou art ever with me, and all that I have is thine.

32 It was meet that we should make merry, and be glad: for this thy brother was dead, and is alive again; and was lost, and is found.

King James Bible

'Your brother has come home'

The prodigal son's homecoming (2)

There was once a man who had two sons; and the younger said to his father, 'Father, give me my share of the property.' So he divided his estate between them. A few days later the younger son turned the whole of his share into cash and left home for a distant country, where he squandered it in reckless living. He had spent it all when a severe famine fell upon that country and he began to feel the pinch. So he went and attached himself to one of the local landlords, who sent him on to his farm to mind the pigs. He would have been glad to fill his belly with the pods that the pigs were eating; and no one gave him anything. Then he came to his senses and said, 'How many of my father's paid servants have more food than they can eat, and here I am starving to death! I will set off and go to my father, and say to him, "Father, I have sinned, against God and against you; I am no longer fit to be your son; treat me as one of your paid servants."'
So he set out for his father's house. But while he was still a long way off his father saw him, and his heart went out to him. He ran to meet him, flung his arms around him, and kissed him. The son said, 'Father, I have sinned, against God and against you; I am no longer fit to be called your son.' But the father said to his servants, 'Quick, bring a robe, my best one, and put it on him; put a ring on his finger and shoes on his feet. Bring the fatted calf and kill it, and let us have a feast to celebrate the day. For this son of mine was dead and has come back to life; he was lost and is found.' And the festivities began.

Now the elder son was out on the farm; and on his way back, as he approached the house, he heard music and dancing. He called one of the servants and asked what it meant. The servant told him, 'Your brother has come home and your father has killed the fatted calf because he has him back safe and sound.' But he was angry and refused to go in. His father came out and pleaded with him; but he retorted, 'You know how I have slaved for you all these years: I never once disobeyed your orders; and you never gave me so much as a kid, for a feast with my friends. But now that this son of yours turns up, after running through

your money with his women, you kill the fatted calf for him.'
'My boy' said the father, 'you are always with me, and everything I have is yours. How could we help celebrating this happy
day? Your brother here was dead and has come back to life, was
lost and is found.'

New English Bible

Questions
What did the younger son do with his share of his inheritance?
What made the younger son come home?
Does the story make clear what the elder son did?
Why was the elder son angry?
What do you think of the younger son?
What do you think of the father?
What do you think of the elder son?
Which of the two accounts do you prefer – the older one or the
modern one?
Where are they the same? How do they differ?
What does *prodigal* mean?
What is a parable? What do you think is the meaning of this
parable?

Discussion
Do you think parents should be allowed to pass on money or
land to their children?

Projects
Find out about *wills* and how they are made. (You might look
to see if your paper ever publishes the amounts some people
leave in their wills.)

Find out how stained glass windows are made.

Writing
Write your own version of the prodigal son's homecoming.
The family and friends are summoned to a reading of a will.
There are some surprises. Tell such a story.

Improvisation

Divide the story into several scenes. Add any details of your own which you consider necessary. Write your own dialogue, and act the scenes.

Art

Look at some biblical stories told in stained glass windows. Make some designs for a stained glass window which tell the story of the prodigal son.

Beowulf—8

Thus Beowulf and his men returned to their ship. This time there was no challenge from the coastguard, and Beowulf honoured him with the gift of a gold-embroidered sword. The ship with the curved prow was loaded with weapons and horses and treasures round the high mast.

Then the boat departed, cutting the deep waters, leaving the Danish coast behind. A sail was hoisted, the timbers creaked, the vessel did not veer from her homeward course as the wind blew over the billows. The ship drove on, a necklace of foam round her proud prow, she rode the waves, the ocean swell, until at last they sighted the cliffs of home, the well-known headlands. With a favourable wind the ship was soon back. A shore sailor, long on the watch for the return of the heroes, quickly seized the mooring ropes and made fast the vessel before the waves could carry the happy home-comers away again. It was not far to heave the treasures to King Hygelac in his high hall.

Thus Beowulf disembarked with his men on the wide sea-beaches of home. The world candle was bright, the sun shining from the south. Beowulf's safe home-coming was made known and the King ordered that preparations be made for their reception. Hygelac welcomed Beowulf. The queen passed round the mead cup. Hygelac asked Beowulf for a full account of his adventures: 'How did it all turn out, beloved Beowulf, when you decided to bear arms far across the waters to bring help to Heorot? Have you had good fortune? I confess I have not been hopeful about the outcome of your expedition. I asked that you should not fight the Spear-Danes' battle for them, and advised you to give Grendel a wide berth. I thank God that you are home safe and sound.'

Beowulf replied: 'King Hygelac, already the account of my dealings with Grendel is famed abroad. No more will he trouble Heorot. But I will enlighten you with some of the details of that struggle. When Grendel attacked us in Heorot he had with him a horrific glove. The glove hung, gaping and gruesome, firmly fixed by cleverly wrought hands. It was all made with great skill and devilish craft, out of the skins of dragons. Without any cause, it was his intention to cram me and as many others as he could into that thing. It would take too long to give you a full account of how I finished him. But shortly he was lifeless at the bottom of the mere.

'Hrothgar rewarded me for my trouble handsomely with beaten gold and many treasures, when we banqueted after the battle. The gleemen sang. Hrothgar told of far-off things of long ago. A warrior played the harp and told sad stories. Hrothgar lamented over the loss of youth and was nostalgic for days gone by. We made merry until night again overtook us. With the night came Grendel's dam to destroy us. But fate was not ready to doom me to death yet. I dealt with Grendel's mother and was again showered with many gifts, which I have brought to you, dear Hygelac, my King.'

Then Beowulf ordered his men to bring in a boar's head banner, a lofty battle-helmet, a grey corselet, and a splendid war sword: 'Hrothgar bequeathed this breast armour as a great heirloom especially to you, Hygelac.' Four bay horses followed these gifts, and to Hygelac's queen was given the priceless necklace.

Thus Beowulf showed what kind of man he was, proved himself as a man of bravery, of honour and of wisdom. He was not the kind of man to get drunk and kill his friends. He was a gentle man, brave in battle, who took care of the gifts God had given to him. For a long time he had been passed over. His people had undervalued his valour and Hygelac had neglected to honour him in the feast hall. They had put him down as idle and unpromising. The record was soon put straight, and brave Beowulf recompensed. Hygelac ordered his father's golden heirloom to be brought in. No sword existed in the land to compare with this treasure. The King presented it to Beowulf, together with a hall of his own, seven thousand hides of land, and a title. They both ruled now in their country, by right.

Dictionary or Discussion
   gleemen
   nostalgic
   heirloom

Invent and relate an episode in Beowulf's youth which might have given rise to the feeling that he was worthless.

For discussion. Rewards.

Find out all about measuring. (What was a hide of land?)

Write a story about a person thought to be worthless, who eventually proves himself.

III (1) Of responsibility

1. *'It kills you'* (*Eleven views on smoking*)
2. *'Now you can go to work'*
3. *'I'm determined to leave everything to you'*
4. *'Up to your games again?'*
5. *'Who was to blame?'*
6. *'Why should I care?'* (*Eleven views on the Crucifixion*)
7. *Beowulf's responsibility for his people*

'It kills you' (Eleven views on smoking)

A teacher describes how these pieces came to be written:

In the lesson (with 13-year-olds) I was asking pupils to come out and give short speeches on selected topics, when one pupil asked if we could talk about smoking. I agreed to this, and discussion followed.

Then I asked them to write down their views.

1. I like to smoke because I can't stop. The cigs I like best are Embassy, tipped and full strength. Embassy are a nice fine tobacco and not so strong. But full strength are the strongest. But the cigs I smoke are not mine, they are other people's. Smoking is a bad habit and a waste of money. They say you can get lung cancer but I haven't had it yet or I wouldn't be writing this now. The nicotine I get on my fingers is of woodies but I rub my fingers on a wall to get rid of it.

2. Smoking is a good habit if you can afford it. It is best to buy woodbines because they are cheap, with a rich virginia blend. My dad smokes woodbines and he won't smoke any other because he is the same as me, a woodbine addict. When he is hard up he rolls his own dockers.

3. I started smoking when I was 11 years old. I smoked Nelson tipped, which were 9½p; as I grew older I changed to Gold Leaf tipped. Now I smoke Embassy or Senior Service tipped which are 11p for a packet of ten. I have been asked if my parents know I smoke. Yes, they do. They say they don't care but if they see me smoking I will regret it. Smoking isn't really a bad habit of mine. I only buy about one packet of ten a week or a fortnight. It just depends if I can afford it because I save most of my spending money for the Youth Club.

Last night at the Youth Club I had a packet of ten Senior Service. I gave Chris and Adrian one and my friend Jean. I had seven myself. This morning I found I had nicotine on my index finger. I enjoy smoking.

4. It is good to smoke. I like Embassy tipped best because they are better and they give you free gift coupons. I saw a right funny

programme last night on bronchitis and it was about chaps dying because of smoke but I don't really think it's true that smoking can kill and it's a shame that big nobs have to stop it.

5. Smoking is a bad habit but lots of people can't stop. The best kind of cigs are tipped ones because they soak most of the nicotine up. I know I smoke but I just do it because I like it and if I wanted I think I could stop. The worst thing about smoking is they are very dear and most people can't afford it. It is a very dangerous habit to get and if people wanted to give it up they ought to demolish all the cigs they got hold of. You can get a lot of very dangerous diseases from smoking such as cancer and bronchitis. If you have been smoking for a long time and then manage to stop you will find out that you get fat. I think people ought to cut down on their cigs.

6. I used to smoke but I have given it up. When I did smoke I used to smoke Embassy tipped. But I have decided not to smoke and to start growing. I can't see why it is not good for you but they always say it gives you lung cancer but I have not had it yet.

I don't like smoking, it is unhealthy and makes you cough. It is bad habit and it costs too much money just to kill yourself. Some people say it calms your nerves but it only makes you want some more. The best way to give up smoking is never start.

7. Most of the kids about my age seem to think that if they smoke it makes them older but I think it is ridiculous, it is the cause of so many people's troubles and it is also bad for the chest. I used to smoke but my parents caught me and I got a good talking to and so I have never smoked since. I was 12 then. I am now nearly 14.

8. Smoking is bad for the health and is a bad habit. Also it is a waste of money. It gives you bad breath and colours your fingers yellow. I personally think that smoking is daft, people only smoke because they think if they don't they're not with the fashion, so give up while you are still young. I of course do not smoke.

9. I gave up smoking on Tuesday because I do not want to get Chronic Bronchitis and die. I have given up smoking for good. There are more men smoke than women and I think they all ought to give up like me. If I start again it will be on a pipe.

10. I do not smoke. Sometimes when I see people smoke at my own age I often think of wanting one. If I did smoke I would not be able to afford it. If I did smoke I would not smoke any other cigarettes but tipped ones. When people smoke it is no use trying to hide it because in time you get nicotine on your fingers. Smoking is a very bad habit. It causes cancer. This is a very bad complaint and is very hard to cure and it can kill. Drugs are sometimes found in cigarettes. Children are often tempted to smoke by older people and the younger children are frightened of the older people.

11. I think smoking is one of the worst habits you can ever get into. It kills you. It is a do it yourself cancer kit. Over half of the population of Great Britain die of lung cancer every year. Cigarettes are made of a queer plant. The leaves are shredded up and put in between a bit of paper and rolled up. Then you waste a match on lighting it. When you have been smoking a little while you get a permanent stain called nicotine. Nicotine is the cigarette tar that is melted out of the tobacco. Also it makes you very tired.

Questions
What are the arguments that the writers of these pieces make in favour of smoking?
What are their arguments against smoking?
Which of these pieces of writing do you most agree with? Why?
Which do you most disagree with? Why?

Discussion
'Because smoking is harmful, cigarette advertisements should be banned.'

Writing
What are your own views on smoking?

Improvisation
Work out a series of brief plays designed to put people off smoking.

Project
How do advertisers try to persuade us to smoke?

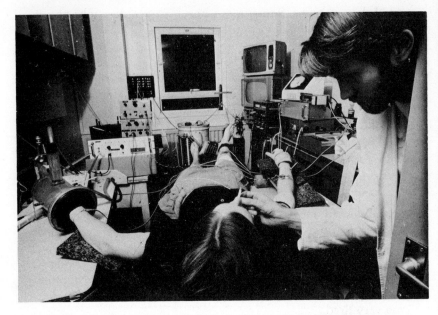

Sunday Times. Ian Yeomans

What does this picture suggest to you? Write a story or description or account of your thoughts or whatever you feel or imagine as you look at it.

Describe the picture as accurately as you can to someone who cannot see it.

'Now you can go to work'

The Easter I was fifteen I sat at the table for supper and Mam said to me: 'I'm glad you've left school. Now you can go to work.'

'I don't want to go to work,' I said in a big voice.

'Well, you've got to,' she said. 'I can't afford to keep a pit-prop like you on nowt.'

I sulked, pushed my toasted cheese away as if it was the worst kind of slop. 'I thought I could have a break before starting.'

'Well, you thought wrong. You'll be out of harm's way at work.' She took my plate and emptied it on John's my younger brother's, knowing the right way to get me mad. That's the trouble with me: I'm not clever. I could have bashed our John's face in and snatched it back, except the little bastard had gobbled it up, and Dad was sitting by the fire, behind his paper with one tab lifted. 'You can't get me out to work quick enough, can you?' was all I could say to Mam.

Dad chipped in, put down his paper. 'Listen: no work, no grub. So get out and look for a job tomorrow, and don't come back till you've got one.'

Going to the bike factory to ask for a job meant getting up early, just as if I was back at school: there didn't seem any point in getting older. My old man was a good worker though, and I knew in my bones and brain that I took after him. At the school garden the teacher used to say: 'Colin, you're the best worker I've got, and you'll get on when you leave' – after I'd spent a couple of hours digging spuds while all the others had been larking about trying to run each other over with the lawn-rollers. Then the teacher would sell the spuds off at threepence a pound and what did I get out of it? Bogger-all. Yet I liked the work because it wore me out; and I always feel pretty good when I'm worn out.

I knew you had to go to work though, and that rough work was best. I saw a picture once about a revolution in Russia, about the workers taking over everybody (like Dad wants to) and they lined everybody up and made them hold their hands out and the working blokes went up and down looking at them. Anybody whose hands was lily-white was taken away and shot. The others was O.K. Well, if ever that happened in this country, I'd be O.K., and that made me feel better when a few days later

I was walking down the street in overalls at half past seven in the morning with the rest of them. One side of my face felt lively and interested in what I was in for, but the other side was crooked and sorry for itself, so that a neighbour got a front view of my whole clock and called with a wide laugh, a gap I'd like to have seen a few inches lower down – in her neck: 'Never mind, Colin, it ain't all that bad.'

ALAN SILLITOE: 'The Bike'

Questions
What kind of picture does this extract give us of Colin's family? (What kind of a boy is Colin? Do you like him? What is his attitude to his mother? To his brother? To his father? To his teacher? To his neighbour? To himself?)

Discussion
'All children should stay at school until they are eighteen.'

Improvisation
Imagine this situation: the teacher calls round at the house and suggests that the boy be allowed to stay on at school. Act two contrasting scenes, (*a*) the discussion that takes place and the way the matter is handled in Colin's family, and (*b*) a discussion and a solution in a different family.

And after all the weather was ideal. They could not have had a more perfect day for a garden party if they had ordered it. Windless, warm, the sky without a cloud. Only the blue was veiled with a haze of light gold, as it is sometimes in early summer.

The gardener had been up since dawn, mowing the lawns and sweeping them, until the grass and the dark flat rosettes where the daisy plants had been seemed to shine. As for the roses, you could not help feeling they understood that roses are the only flowers that impress people at garden parties; the only flowers that everybody is certain of knowing. Hundreds, yes, literally hundreds, had come out in a single night; the green bushes bowed down as though they had been visited by archangels.

Breakfast was not yet over before the men came to put up the marquee.

'Where do you want the marquee put, mother?'

'My dear child, it's no use asking me. I'm determined to leave everything to you children this year. Forget I am your mother. Treat me as an honoured guest.'

But Meg could not possibly go and supervise the men. She had washed her hair before breakfast, and she sat drinking her coffee in a green turban, with a dark wet curl stamped on each cheek. Jose, the butterfly, always came down in a silk petticoat and a kimono jacket.

'You'll have to go, Laura; you're the artistic one.'

Away Laura flew, still holding her piece of bread-and-butter. It's so delicious to have an excuse for eating out of doors, and besides, she loved having to arrange things; she always felt she could do it so much better than anybody else.

Four men in their shirt-sleeves stood grouped together on the garden path. They carried staves covered with rolls of canvas, and they had big tool-bags slung on their backs. They looked impressive. Laura wished now that she was not holding that piece of bread-and-butter, but there was nowhere to put it, and she couldn't possibly throw it away. She blushed and tried to look severe and even a little bit short-sighted as she came up to them.

'Good morning,' she said, copying her mother's voice. But that sounded so fearfully affected that she was ashamed, and stammered like a little girl, 'Oh – er – have you come – is it about the marquee?'

'That's right, miss,' said the tallest of the men, a lanky, freckled fellow, and he shifted his tool-bag, knocked back his straw hat, and smiled down at her. 'That's about it.'

His smile was so easy, so friendly, that Laura recovered. What nice eyes he had, small, but such a dark blue! And now she looked at the others, they were smiling too. 'Cheer up, we won't bite,' their smile seemed to say. How very nice workmen were! And what a beautiful morning! She mustn't mention the morning; she must be business-like. The marquee.

'Well, what about the lily-lawn? Would that do?'

And she pointed to the lily-lawn with the hand that didn't hold the bread-and-butter. They turned, they stared in the direction. A little fat chap thrust out his under-lip, and the tall fellow frowned.

'I don't fancy it,' said he. 'Not conspicuous enough. You see, with a thing like a marquee,' and he turned to Laura in his easy way, 'you want to put it somewhere where it'll give you a bang slap in the eye, if you follow me.'

Laura's upbringing made her wonder for a moment whether it was quite respectful of a workman to talk to her of bangs slap in the eye. But she did quite follow him.

'A corner of the tennis-court,' she suggested. 'But the band's going to be in one corner.'

'H'm, going to have a band, are you?' said another of the workmen. He was pale. He had a haggard look as his dark eyes scanned the tennis-court. What was he thinking?

'Only a very small band,' said Laura gently. Perhaps he wouldn't mind so much if the band was quite small. But the tall fellow interrupted.

'Look here, miss, that's the place. Against those trees. Over there. That'll do fine.'

Against the karakas. Then the karaka-trees would be hidden. And they were so lovely, with their broad, gleaming leaves, and their clusters of yellow fruit. They were like trees you imagined growing on a desert island, proud, solitary, lifting their leaves and fruits to the sun in a kind of silent splendour. Must they be hidden by a marquee?

They must. Already the men had shouldered their staves and were making for the place. Only the tall fellow was left. He bent down, pinched a sprig of lavender, put his thumb and forefinger to his nose and snuffed up the smell. When Laura saw that gesture she forgot all about the karakas in her wonder at him caring for things like that – caring for the smell of lavender. How many men that she knew would have done such a thing? Oh, how extraordinarily nice workmen were, she thought. Why couldn't she have workmen for friends rather than the silly boys she danced with and who came to Sunday night supper? She would get on much better with men like these.

KATHERINE MANSFIELD: *The Garden Party and Other Stories*

Questions
Why couldn't Meg supervise the men?
What do you think of Laura?
What do you think the pale workman might have been thinking?
How did the tall fellow surprise Laura?

Improvisation
After the previous extract ('Now you can go to work'), two scenes were suggested about a boy discussing staying on at school. Now invent two scenes about a girl who wants to leave school at the age of 15, though her family want her to stay on. In one of the scenes, involve the characters from this extract. In the other, choose characters from a different family.

Discussion
Not a great many pupils organize garden parties of the kind being planned here. Not many of us live the lives of the fictitious characters we enjoy reading about. Did you enjoy reading this extract? Can you suggest reasons, even if you don't like this particular extract, why we enjoy reading about people different from ourselves? Why do we sometimes enjoy very 'sad' stories? Do you prefer 'serious' stories to 'comedies'?

Writing
Complete the story of the garden party.
Whom would you rather meet—Colin (page 205) or Laura? Describe your imaginary meeting. Describe a meeting between Colin and Laura.

'Who was to blame?'

I am the one responsible

It is dark. A man's voice can be heard: 'It's not much to ask. I've never asked for a lot. I shouldn't have got it anyway. Whatever I wanted. . . . A little light. Just a glimmer. Just enough to see to die by. . . ' (*The moon comes out. We see the man who is talking. He is a wisp of a man, in an old macintosh several sizes too large for him. He is wearing a brown paper bag over his head. He goes on talking:*)

'Oh, that's too sudden. I don't want to die suddenly. Not like all the others, whisped out in a puff. But I don't want to die slowly either. A man ought to have the right to die the way he wants. It should be easy. A piece of string, an old razor blade, an overdose of aspirin. . . . But what's the use? Why take all the responsibility when a falling brick might do as well? Why die at all? Why live at all? Why sit here asking questions? . . . I'm hungry. . . . Oh, it's not fair. The fools in authority make mistakes, and who has to suffer? Who? There should be no fools in authority. There should be no authority. A man should be left to himself. . . . I don't want to be left to myself. Dust. All that's left. Dust. All my hopes. All my chances. Dust. Dust. Dust. Dust. . . .'

(*The world is supposed to have been devastated by the atom bomb. He is the only survivor, he believes, saved by his brown paper bag. Who is to blame for it all? As he is thinking about it, a smartly dressed girl with a good figure walks by. Over her head she wears a brown paper bag. They talk:*)

MAN: Perhaps I ought to introduce myself.

GIRL: Please do.

MAN: My name is Phythick. I am – a schoolmaster.

GIRL: Oh, yes?

MAN: I teach physics and higher mathematics. I – taught – physics and higher mathematics. I am quite attached to mathematics. They dispense with words, you see. They are like unemotional music. Sine over cosine equals tangent. No confusion there. I was a comparatively successful teacher. A few of my pupils became chiefs of nuclear research. One was actually knighted. Another was responsible for important developments in heterodynamic deterrents. He – he always thought it possible to reduce living organisms to dust – by remote control. I am not responsible for my pupils though. I merely pass on knowledge, you understand. It is up to them what they do with it. Most of them become butchers, brokers, or insurance agents. I am not responsible if they advance their careers in heterodynamic deterrents.

GIRL: Of course not.

MAN: Do you think so? Do you really think so?

GIRL: Of course. You just told me so.

MAN: Do you believe everything you're told?

GIRL: Don't you?

MAN: I – try to strike a balance. . . . Who are you? What is your name?

GIRL: You don't know? It doesn't show?

MAN: A great deal shows, but not your name.

GIRL: I'm Miss Europe.

MAN: Miss Europe?

GIRL: This year's Miss Europe. I'd have been Miss World next year, only now there doesn't seem to be a world to be Miss of.

MAN: Don't you wonder which fool allowed this to happen? Didn't you ask yourself who was to blame?

GIRL: I didn't know anyone allowed it. I thought it just happened – like a wet Bank Holiday.

MAN: Oh, no. Oh, no, no, no, no, no, no. Whitehall blundered. They gave the fanatics in heterodynamic deterrents carte blanche. Can you imagine that? They deputed absolute authority for the world to be destroyed.

(*Gradually they become attached to each other:*)

MAN: Miss Europe . . . I want you to understand that this is no hurried statement. Although it may appear to be composed on the spur of the moment, it has a lifetime's reasoning behind it.

GIRL: I know perfectly well what you are going to say, and I might as well tell you here and now that I agree with every word of it.

MAN: The very act of living involves us in responsibility. We cannot cross a street without affecting the lives of others. There is more responsibility than a single person can bear.

GIRL: O, Mr Thing. . . .

MAN: I warm towards you. Do you know that? I have feelings

surging in me that hardly become a mathematics master. I want to crush my lips against your rosebud mouth. . . . Is it a rosebud mouth?

GIRL: It's not very large.

MAN: You – must have a pretty face.

GIRL: I thought so once.

MAN: You do – have a face?

GIRL: You tell me.

MAN: How can I? I've never seen it.

GIRL: How do I know I've a face at all if you won't tell me?

MAN: How do I know what face you've got when it's hidden under a bag?

GIRL: Shall I take it off?

MAN: No. Why are you trying to push responsibility onto me?

GIRL (*Accusingly*): You're afraid.

MAN: What more is there to say?

GIRL: Nothing. Just cuddle close to me.

(*They do that. Their heads touch. The brown paper bags crinkle. They sit sharply upright.*)

GIRL: We crinkled.

MAN: We were bound to. Paper does crinkle.

GIRL: Paper tears.

(*Pause*)

MAN: It's dangerous.

GIRL: We mustn't sit too closely, or kiss, or rub our bags together or anything.

MAN: We might tear.

GIRL (*Tearfully*): It's difficult – being in love. Isn't it?

MAN: We do love each other, don't we?

GIRL: We need each other.

MAN (*Hopelessly*): We can always hold hands.

(*Pause*)

GIRL: I thought people in love always did things. Like lie in the long grass, or nibble each other's ears.

MAN: We're different.

(*Pause*)

GIRL: We shall never really come together, shall we? We shall never know each other as two people ought to know each other.

MAN: Never.

GIRL: Never?

MAN: Never.
GIRL: Not as long as we wear these bags.
MAN: Not until I'm unafraid.
GIRL: Not until I understand.
  (*Pause*)
GIRL: We shall always wear these bags. . . . Shan't we?
MAN: Of course. Unless. . . .
GIRL: Yes?
  (*Pause*)
MAN (*An idea stirring*): We. . . .
GIRL (*Hope dawning*): Go on. . . .
MAN: Then. . . . (*He raises his hands to his bag.*)
  (*A cloud comes over the moon.*)

DAVID CAMPTON: *The Lunatic View*

Questions
Whom does the man blame for the catastrophe which is supposed
to have happened?
Whom does the girl blame?
Why won't the man agree to the girl taking off her paper bag?
What do you think the man is going to do as the cloud comes
over the moon?

Discussion
What part can the individual play in world affairs? (Do you
believe in marches? Letters to the newspapers? Should you be
able to vote at 16? At 13?)
In what ways can 12/13-year-olds be 'responsible'?
In what ways can they be irresponsible?

Writing
'We cannot cross a street without affecting the lives of others.'
In what ways do *you* affect the lives of others?

Drama
Read this play extract.
(The destruction of the human race by atomic warfare is a
serious topic. Does the playwright succeed in making you laugh
about it? What kind of laughter is it?)

Imperial War Museum

What does this picture suggest to you? Write a story or description or account of your thoughts or whatever you feel or imagine as you look at it.

Give the picture a title.

Write a poem about it called 'The Last Survivor'.

'Why should I care?'

Eleven Views of the Crucifixion

1. *Captain of the Guards*
   I enjoy my job,
   You may say I'm cruel,
   So what.
   I don't care,
   Why should I care?
   I'm 'The Captain of the Guard'.

2. *A Soldier*
   I saw the Christ carrying his cross up the hill of Golgotha.
   He dropped the cross. I did not yell, but gave
   It to someone else to carry.
   And then I told him to hurry.

   People were weeping, I did not like the job,
   But I knew I had to do it, or I would die
   And if I refused to do it someone else would try.
   He did not groan as I nailed him down by his
   Hands and by his feet.
   And I put a crown of thorns on his head to make
   The High Priests laugh.

   The High Priests laughed in a discreet way
   For this was a big day.
   A lifetime past in a few hours' time and
   Christ was dead.
   But my captain went to finish him off, he
   Pierced his side and I could not watch.
   But I did not like the job that day
   But I had to do it.

3. *A Robber*
   I had only robbed to get food,
   And now I was being crucified for it.

They roped my hands to the beams
And my legs too,
My cross was then jerked into position.
Another robber like myself was also being crucified that
    same day.
And so was another man,
He was called Jesus Christ
Known as the Son of God.

He was treated so harshly
Sharp nails were driven through his bare hands
And one through his 'crossed feet'
Blood trickled down his body to the ground
While his head lay drooping
Still covered with the crown of thorns.

I couldn't understand why *he* was to be crucified
What had he done wrong?
Surely a man like Jesus could never do anything wrong
Had the people or his disciples turned against him?
I couldn't understand it at all.

Many people came to watch the crucifixions,
I saw his mother crying,
If he claimed to be King of the Jews,
Why had he not brought himself down from the cross?
This puzzled me.

The sky began to grow dark
Our time was drawing near,
He hadn't spoken much
Only a murmur now and again,
I now began to feel very weak and weary.

I asked him for a pardon
As I was not too far away from him,
He accepted it
I thanked him, I felt so free of my sins,
I could now die in peace. . . .

4. *Judas Iscariot*

I Judas Iscariot, the man who betrayed Jesus
I am stood watching Jesus on the cross
Why did I do it
Please tell me please
Maybe because I wanted money
No I have money enough
Well why did I do it
Please tell me please
Maybe because I was jealous of him
No I loved him dearly
Why did I do it
Please tell me please
Maybe because I hated him
No I loved him dearly
I do not know
I do not know
Why did I do it
Please tell me please
Maybe because I was jealous of the other disciples
Because he loved them more than me
No he loved us all
Maybe I will kill myself if I do
Not find out
Oh forgive me Lord
Forgive me
Oh please, please please
Forgive me
Why did I do it
Please tell me please
I will kill myself if I do not find out why
Why
Oh why.

5. *Mary Mother of Jesus*

They lashed him, and blood ran down his back.
He carried his own cross that he was going to die on,
His face was pale his body was weak,
Why did they do this to him,
Why did they do this to my Son.

He was a good man and I loved him,
He had given the blind their eyes to see,
He had given the deaf their hearing back,
He had given the dumb their speech back,
So why why, do they want to kill him.

He's not a king as kings go,
But in my eyes and in the eyes of other good people,
See him as a king a godly king,
But now they are going to kill him—nail him to a cross.

There he is dying on the Holy Cross
Blood running down his hands and feet,
But I know he is dying, but I will see him again
In Heaven with God.

6. *Mary Magdalene*
   I was a sinner until Jesus came,
   He freed me from all my sins,
   That day I was to see him die,
   I could have died too,
   I watched him stagger up the hill,
   With the heavy burden of a cross,
   They highered him—he was high above our heads,
   He died for many people who were sinners like me,
   But they never took any notice.

7. *A Disciple of Christ*
   It was a blazing hot day when Jesus was to die
   He dragged his eight foot cross, like a
   Lame ass through the streets of Jerusalem,
   Then the soldiers dragged a man out of
   The crowd to carry it for him.
   It was taken to Mt Golgotha where
   Jesus had big nails driven through his wrists,
   The cross was stood upright,
   And the blood ran like raging streams
   Down his body.
   In about three hours the guards and soldiers came back
   I reckon the soldier thought he was dead.
   So he gave him a gentle stab in the side.
   He didn't give a cry,
   Like some of them do.

8. *A Disciple of Christ*
   I ran away,
   I left him there alone, alone with the High Priest and
      soldiers.
   That Judas, he was there,
   He kissed him.
   What a way to betray him,
   The priest came with the soldiers
   That Judas, he was there,
   They took Christ Jesus away from us,
   They took him to be judged
   That Judas, he was there.

9. *Joseph of Arimathaea*
   I am Joseph of Arimathaea,
   It is a blazing hot day
   The beloved Son of God has been crucified
   On the cross,
   I have to carry him to the tomb
   I didn't want to do it
   I had seen Jesus crucified it was horrible
   The blood dripping down his body
   Onto his feet
   There were many people there
   My mouth was very dry as I carried him
   To the tomb, which was far away
   I thought if he could really be the Son of God,
   If he was, he could have saved himself.
   Many people owed their lives to him.

10. *Simon of Cyrene*
    I watched the man called Christ pass by. On that hot
    summer's day. I saw him fall not once but twice under the
    burden of the cross. He says he is the son of God and some-
    thing inside of me says it's true. He fell again under the cross
    and with great shouts I was dragged and ordered to carry
    it for him. I protested but somehow I felt that I was doing
    good in helping him. There were cheers and shouts as I
    trudged along with that heavy cross until we got to the place.
    Two people were up already on crosses. Then as I left that
    hill three crosses lined the horizon. They cheered rebuked
    and ridiculed him yet they called him THE SON OF GOD.

11. *One of the Disciples*
    At the crucifixion they smashed in his legs,
    They hit him until his legs were broken,
    They watched him hang there,
    Until the blood disappeared,
    And smote him until he was dead.
    I watched him also hanging right there,
    Wondering why he couldn't escape
    He spoke about his lord and saviour
    He spoke also of me
    And also of thee
    And then of the thieves who were hanged.

Improvisation
These poems were written by pupils who had been acting the
story of the Crucifixion. Use some of the characters in making
your own play.

Albright-Knox Art Gallery, Buffalo, New York

Describe this picture as accurately as you can.

Write an account of your thoughts and feelings as you look at it.
Give it a title.

Do you find anything unusual or surprising about the picture?
Describe how you would colour it.

Find some other pictures by Gauguin. Do you like his work?
Do you like this picture? Find a colour reproduction of it. Does
it lose or gain anything by being in colour?

Do you think Gauguin the artist was trying to say anything in
the picture?

Beowulf—9

The story tells how troubles break out again. A long time ago, the last survivor of a tribe buried a hoard of treasures in the earth. A dragon discovered this hoard and mounted guard over it, where it remained untouched for many years. But one day, while the dragon was sleeping, a man who was escaping from the law discovered the treasure, and stole some of it so that he could perhaps use it to buy his peace with his lord. When the dragon awoke he was enraged at the theft.

Time passed, battles raged, and Hygelac died. Eventually, all the land was left to Beowulf's care. Beowulf ruled it well for fifty winters. Then a dragon was roused from its treasure hoard.

This is how it happened. In far-off days, a man, seeing the passing of all his people, and awaiting the same fate, determined to protect for as long as he might the prized possessions and treasures of his folk. There was a barrow he knew by the seashore, an ideal hiding-place all ready, and protected with old spells. The survivor of his race carried to this hiding-place the treasures and the beaten gold. When he had interred the riches, he said these words: 'Have now and hold, earth, those treasures which men could not keep. Once upon a time it was all taken from you. Death and war's destruction destroyed all my people. Now I have no one to swing the sword, or to polish the golden cup. My warriors have gone. Now will the hardy helmet, gold adorned, lose its golden glory. Those who should take care of the casques are now asleep. The armour, too, which stood up to the strokes of battle, when shields smashed together, perishes like those who have worn it. The corselets are still and travel no more into battle. There is no one to play the harp or lute. No good hawk whirs through the hall. No swift steed stamps on the castle stones. Baleful death has destroyed human life.' So the solitary survivor lamented, alone until his turn also came and the tide of death rose over him. Only the treasure hoard was left.

It was fated that the ancient enemy of man should find the deserted treasure hoard. The scaly, evil Dragon, terror of the night, who flies in the shadows seeking treasure barrows, terrifying the country folk, lit upon the wide open hoard. There, spitefully and selfishly, he kept watch over the gold which he could not use. For three hundred years he had slept over this treasure. Then, a fugitive from justice, who chanced upon the hoard, stole a precious cup, with which he hoped to buy his pardon. The barrow was ransacked and the Dragon enraged. As soon as the great Worm roused himself from sleep he discovered the tracks where the robber had crept close by his head. Round and round the barrow searched the Dragon, alight with fury, burning and flaming for revenge. When he discovered the extent of the loss over and above the stolen goblet, he could scarce contain himself till nightfall. Swollen with fury, he planned to punish with fire the race of men. As night fell he set forth, spewing flame and fury. It started badly for the country folk, but it turned out even worse for their protector, Beowulf. And he did not have to wait long.

The evil Serpent lost no time in burning the bright houses; the flames leapt to the sky, a terror to mortals. The flying horror left no thing in his path alive. The Worm's warfare was brought home to all, people both far and wide felt his fury and spite. Before daybreak he returned to his barrow, having laid waste the surrounding country with flame, fire and inferno. He felt safe within his walls, secure in his strength. His faith was ill founded. Beowulf soon knew the sad story, and the truth struck home bitterly when he learnt that his own home, the best of buildings, the royal palace, had melted away before the surge of the Dragon's fire. It caused him great distress. He thought he had offended God and sank into a despondent mood.

The flaming Dragon had laid waste the people's fortress, and all the surrounding seaboard. Beowulf now planned revenge. The protector of his people ordered that a glorious battle-shield be got ready for him, all in iron. He was aware that no wood, no linden shield could survive those stabbing flames. The renowned prince of his people was nearing the end of his life in this world, and the Dragon as well, though he had guarded the treasure hoard for so long.

Beowulf despised the air-raiding enemy, and disdained to seek him out with an army of men. He had no fear of the fight for himself, and he did not rate highly the Worm's warfare, or its staying power. He had come through too much since he had freed Hrothgar's hall and destroyed Grendel's dam. But he took with him twelve others, bristling with anger, to spy out the Dragon's lair. He had by now discovered how the Dragon had been roused – the fugitive who had stolen the cup had given it to Beowulf. This robber, the cause of the present destruction, made up the thirteenth man of the band. Much against his will he had to return to point out the barrow close by the grumbling sea, the hidden vaults by the surge, crammed with precious treasures, guarded by the Dragon who had grown old watching beneath the ground. It was not an easy job to get past him.

Beowulf addressed his retainers. His spirits were downcast, he was ill at ease and had a premonition of death. Fate was waiting close round the corner to shake the old man's hand, receive his precious soul and take the life from his body. Soon his spirit would be released from its earthly flesh.

'I have seen old men suffering the sight of their own sons swinging on the gallows. They keen over their child's body which feeds the ravens, and they are helpless in their old age. Each new day reminds them of their grief, and they have no great desire to see the destruction of a second son. Heartbroken, they gaze upon their children's homes, empty banqueting halls, hosts only of winds and misery. The horsemen sleep, the heroes in their graves. The harp lies still and all is joyless where once was great mirth.

'So they go and lament alone. Every space is wide and empty. Now, in my old age, I must accept my responsibility and fate, and take my sword to this Dragon who stands watch over the treasure hoard.'

Dictionary or Discussion
    barrow (in the sense of 'an ancient mound')
    interred
    casques
    seaboard
    linden
    premonition
    keen (in the sense of 'making a funeral song')

Are there any ways in which you think that this description is more pessimistic or sombre than the earlier descriptions of Beowulf when he accepted responsibility for keeping Heorot safe for Hrothgar against Grendel? (Do you feel Beowulf will win? Does his old age affect his outlook? Are there any other factors? What has 'fate' to do with it?)

For discussion. 'Kings, prime ministers, presidents, generals and schoolteachers should retire at the age of forty.'

What do you understand by 'the ancient enemy of man'?

Write the story of a family bereaved of their eldest child.

Compose a poem called 'The Song of the Last Survivor'.

Play reading. The Thwarting of Baron Bolligrew by Robert Bolt.

Make a collection of *illustrations* of dragons.

How would you make a dragon for a play?

III (2) **Of bravery**

The horse without a head

Gaby and the rest of the gang were there in front of Fernand Douin's house at the top of the rue des Petits-Pauvres. One after another, the ten children mounted their horse and shot down the hill at top speed to the rue de la Vache Noire at the bottom. There the rider jumped to the ground and ran back up the slope dragging his steed behind him, to where his friends were impatiently waiting their turn.

Ever since Marion, the girl with the dogs, had knocked down old Monsieur Gédéon as he was crossing the rue Cécile, they had posted little Bonbon at the cross-roads to hold up passers-by and to warn the gang if traffic were coming. The horse shot down the rue des Petits-Pauvres, making the most appalling noise from its three iron wheels. It was wonderful, and the cross-roads gave the ride a spice of danger that made it even more glorious. Then, right at the very end, the road made a steep climb, taking the horse and rider on to the bank round the Clos Pecqueux. As you breasted the rise you could see nothing but empty fields stretching grey to the horizon, so that for two seconds you felt as though you were flying. But if you failed to brake with your heels, in a flash you were over the crupper and flat on your back. When this happened the children called it a 'three-point landing'. At the end of each ride the horse toppled over on the kerb and its sides gave a hollow, mournful thump as they hit the hard cobblestones. No run was ever the same.

Fernand Douin had owned the horse for nearly a year. A rag-and-bone merchant from the Faubourg-Bacchus had exchanged it with Monsieur Douin for three packets of black tobacco, and Fernand had found it standing by his stocking on Christmas morning. For five whole minutes he had been too overcome with joy to utter a word. And yet to all outward appearance there was nothing very grand about the horse. It had never, even in the beginning, had a proper head, for although Monsieur Douin had stuck on a rough-and-ready cardboard affair, that hadn't lasted for more than two days. Marion had knocked it off on her first ride as she swept down at forty miles an hour into the back of Monsieur Mazurier's coal lorry. The head and the forelegs (the other casualties) were left behind in the gutter. Then the hind legs were snapped off short when the children rather rashly made a trial run through the tunnel on the Ponceau road. There is no need to tell you about the tail – there had never been one. All they now had left was the body, dapple grey under flaking varnish, with a little brown saddle painted on it. The rag-and-bone man had thrown in an old tricycle under-carriage – without either pedals or chain, it is true, but then you can't have everything. And there it was; a horse on three iron wheels that ran like a thoroughbred down the tarmac slope of the rue des Petits-Pauvres.

The children from Cité Ferrand were green with envy and said that this horse, a horse in the barest essentials, might just as well be a donkey or a pig (pig, they said, described it better than anything); and they asserted that the cowboys of the rue des Petits-Pauvres had no business to play the fool and risk their necks on an old pig with no head. For there was no denying that breaking the horse in had been a tough job. Fernand had lost most of one knee on the fence round César Aravant's scrap-yard; Marion had left a couple of teeth in the Ponceau tunnel, and it hadn't been very pleasant for either of them. But the knee got well in three days and second teeth had come through in a fort-night, and the horse still worked. And worked well, even by the standards of the smoky little back streets where nearly every man worked on the railways and kept the trains running.

After long negotiations it had eventually been agreed that the gang should use the horse once a day, so as to avoid putting too much strain upon it, each member getting two rides. No one had given the horse a long life, even by reducing the running time like this, until Easter was the longest anyone had hoped for, but despite the most fearsome spills, it had held together, and still took you hell for leather down the rue des Petits-Pauvres. Gaby, the only one to cover the whole course without once putting on the 'brakes', had the record down to thirty-five seconds.

It was thanks to the horse that Fernand had been able to enrol his friend Marion in Gaby's gang, the closest of all the secret societies in Louvigny-Triage.

Being the only ones to take part in this daring sport had drawn the group even closer together. Gaby had purposely kept the numbers down and never accepted anyone over twelve, for, as he said, 'Once you're over twelve you become a complete fool and you're lucky if you don't stay like that for the rest of your life.' It was rather awkward, however, since Gaby himself was threatened by the age limit; but he secretly planned to raise it to fourteen and so benefit by this slight reprieve.

Now Tatave, little Bonbon's elder brother, was about to set off under the critical gaze of his friends.

'Look how heavy he is,' said Marion to Fernand. 'He shouldn't have more than one go, really. One of these days your horse will collapse under that great fat lump, and we'll see it coming up again with the wheels all squashed.'

A hundred yards below, little Bonbon, watching the junction of the rue Cécile, waved the all clear. Tatave shot past him like a rocket, head down, hands riveted to the rusty handle-bars of the horse.

'He's got the weight,' shrugged Juan, the little Spanish boy. 'But he'll never beat Gaby. He's a funk. Puts on the brakes fifty yards away from the rue de la Vache Noire. What we ought to do one day is to shove him off with his legs tied under the handle-bars.'

Farther on, the rue des Petits-Pauvres curved round out of sight of the watchers. They waited, but not for long. A great crash of breaking glass came up from the end of the road, then a wail, a flurry of curses, and the sharp crack of two good slaps.

'Crikey!' muttered Gaby, his jaw tightening, 'Tatave's had a smash!'

'Let's have a look,' suggested Fernand, who was rather worried about the horse.

'Zidore and Mélie stayed at the bottom,' said Marion; 'they'll get him out of any jam without our bothering.'

Gaby automatically glanced round. Apart from Marion, Fernand, and Juan, there was Berthe Gédéon, and Criquet Lariqué, the little darky from the Faubourg-Bacchus.

'We'll go as far as the rue Cécile,' he said. 'We can't leave them on their own; there may have been a real accident.'

When they got to the cross-roads they saw the others coming round the corner, their looks as gloomy as the dull December day. Zidore Loche was pulling the unfortunate horse along on two wheels, while beside him walked Tatave, limping slightly, rather red in the face and carrying the third wheel in his hand. Amélie Babin, the gang's first-aid expert, brought up the rear grinning from ear to ear and shaking with suppressed laughter. Every now and then she turned round to look down the rue des Petits-Pauvres, whence came strangled sounds of rage.

'It was bound to happen sooner or later!' cried Zidore as he came up. 'He always brakes at the wrong moment. Old Zigon was coming up from the main road with his hand-cart loaded with bottles just as Tatave comes round the bend. I stayed put, but what does Tatave do? Jams on his brakes and *smack!* Slap into the cart!'

Mélie rocked with laughter; her thin little face, framed by a black scarf over her fair hair, was split by a wicked grin.

'Tatave made a lovely three-point landing. You should have seen him! He went like a bomb right over the wire round the Clos. Honest! Old Zigon stood gaping like a cod-fish.'

'The old boy's O.K.?' asked Gaby.

'Yes, but a couple of dozen bottles got smashed and he's in an awful temper.'

'We'll bring him five dozen tomorrow evening,' said Marion. 'There's a whole stack of them in the pit behind the old trucks in the siding. No one else knows the place.'

Tatave had grazed his left knee badly and the seat of his trousers was plastered with thick yellow mud.

'Buckets and buckets and *buckets* of blood,' he muttered angrily.

Shamefacedly he handed the wheel to Fernand, while the others crowded round Zidore to examine the horse. Fifi, Marion's favourite dog, sniffed disdainfully at the cut and her dented wooden carcass.

'Well, this really looks as though we've had it now,' said Gaby, looking up in consternation. 'The front fork's snapped clean off; there are the two ends on the wheel. You've made a jolly good job of it, Tatave, I must say!'

Tatave blushed, hung his head, and sniffed.

The weight of the disaster silenced them all for a minute. Fernand's heart sank. His horse! There was nothing like it from Louvigny to Villeneuve-Saint-Georges. Marion slid her hand on to his shoulder.

'Your father will fix it for you,' she whispered. 'After all, it's not the first time it's happened.'

'I don't know,' Fernand replied, shaking his head; 'the fork's broken, and you know what that means; it's a really big job to repair it.'

Then little Bonbon came up from the rue Cécile, crying his eyes out.

'It's always the same!' he bellowed. 'I haven't had my second turn and you go and bust up the horse. . . .'

Gaby turned to comfort the baby of the gang.

'Don't cry, Bonbon. Next time you shall have three goes instead of two.'

'My eye!' howled Bonbon, 'there won't be a next time. The horse is smashed to bits.'

Tatave, quite overwhelmed, tried to make himself as small as possible. Desperately he explained, 'When I saw old Zigon come up on the left I jammed on the brakes. Anyone would have done the same.'

'Oh yes!' retorted Gaby. 'You jammed on the brakes and went straight into him! You poor fool, the last thing you should have done was to put the brakes on.'

All the children giggled except Marion and Fernand, who picked up the wheel in one hand, the handle-bars in the other, and climbed slowly home, dragging the horse behind him. The others lagged behind, hands in pockets, discussing the accident.

PAUL BERNA: *A Hundred Million Francs*

Questions
Who was the owner of the 'horse'?
What was the 'history' of the horse?
Describe the 'horse', and how it was made.
Who held the record on the 'horse'?
What was the record?
What exactly happened to the 'horse'?
What hope was there for it?

Project
'Street and playground games.'

Writing
Write a story about another makeshift 'animal'.
Write a letter to a friend, as though you had witnessed the accident, and describe in the letter what you saw.

Discussion

'Once you're over twelve you become a complete fool and you're lucky if you don't stay like that for the rest of your life.'

Improvisation

The 'horse' visits one of the gang in a dream. What does the horse say?

The School You Would Like?

Yes, school is not just a world full of teachers teaching dopey children, children must co-operate as well, and the school should be a happy place.

ROSEMARY, 13

One last thing, the playgrounds. These are for both girls and boys. They may fight, but if a boy cannot be allowed to be with a girl, then when he grows up, he will be downright shy of them (when first meeting a girl), or be rotten to them.

ANTONY, 13, and CHRISTOPHER, 13

Reproduced from *A Country Camera* by Gordon Winter

What does this picture suggest to you? Write a story or description or account of your thoughts or whatever you feel or imagine as you look at it.

Write an adventure involving the characters in this photo and in the previous extract. Invent more characters and 'machines' if you like. Put yourself into the story if you wish.

As the young man came over the hill the first thin blowing of rain met him. . . . He stopped.

Over to his right a thin, black horse was running across the ploughland towards the hill, its head down, neck stretched out. It seemed to be running on its toes like a cat, like a dog up to no good.

From the high point on which he stood the hill dipped slightly and rose to another crested point fringed with the tops of trees, three hundred yards to his right. As he watched it, the horse ran up to that crest, showed against the sky – for a moment like a nightmarish leopard – and disappeared over the other side.

For several seconds he stared at the skyline, stunned by the unpleasantly strange impression the horse had made on him. Then the plastering beat of icy rain on his bare skull brought him to himself. The distance had vanished in a wall of grey. All around him the fields were jumping and streaming. . . .

He wanted this rain to go on forever. Whenever it seemed to be drawing off he listened anxiously until it closed in again. As long as it lasted he was suspended from life and time. He didn't want to return to his sodden shoes and his possibly ruined suit and the walk back over that land of mud.

All at once he shivered. He hugged his knees to squeeze out the cold and found himself thinking of the horse. The hair on the nape of his neck prickled slightly. He remembered how it had run up to the crest and showed against the sky.

He tried to dismiss the thought. Horses wander about the countryside often enough. But the image of the horse as it had appeared against the sky stuck in his mind. It must have come over the crest just above the wood in which he was now sitting. To clear his mind, he twisted around and looked up the wood between the tree stems, to his left.

At the wood top, with the silvered grey light coming in behind it, the black horse was standing under the oaks, its head high and alert, its ears pricked, watching him.

A horse sheltering from the rain generally goes into a sort of stupor, tilts a hind hoof and hangs its head and lets its eyelids droop, and so it stays as long as the rain lasts. This horse was nothing like that. It was watching him intently, standing perfectly still, its soaked neck and flank shining in the hard light.

He turned back. His scalp went icy and he shivered. What was he to do? Ridiculous to try driving it away. And to leave the wood, with the rain still coming down full pelt, was out of the question. Meanwhile the idea of being watched became more and more unsettling until at last he had to twist around again, to see if the horse had moved. It stood exactly as before.

This was absurd. He took control of himself and turned back deliberately, determined not to give the horse one more thought. If it wanted to share the wood with him, let it. If it wanted to stare at him, let it. He was nestling firmly into these resolutions when the ground shook and he heard the crash of a heavy body coming down the wood. Like lightning his legs bounded him upright and about face. The horse was almost on top of him, its head stretching forwards, ears flattened and lips lifted back from the long yellow teeth. He got one snapshot glimpse of the red-veined eyeball as he flung himself backwards around the tree. Then he was away up the slope, whipped by oak twigs as he leapt the brambles and brushwood, twisting between the close trees till he tripped and sprawled. As he fell the warning flashed through his head that he must at all costs keep his suit out of the leaf-mould, but a more urgent instinct was already rolling him violently sideways. He spun around, sat up and looked back, ready to scramble off in a flash to one side. He was panting from the sudden excitement and effort. The horse had disappeared. The wood was empty except for the drumming, slant grey rain, dancing the bracken and glittering from the branches.

He got up, furious. Knocking the dirt and leaves from his suit as well as he could he looked around for a weapon. The horse was evidently mad, had an abscess on its brain or something of the sort. Or maybe it was just spiteful. Rain sometimes puts creatures into queer states. Whatever it was, he was going to get away from the wood as quickly as possible, rain or no rain.

Since the horse seemed to have gone on down the wood, his way to the farm over the hill was clear. As he went, he broke a yard length of wrist-thick dead branch from one of the oaks, but immediately threw it aside and wiped the slime of rotten wet bark from his hands with his soaked handkerchief. Already he was thinking it incredible that the horse could have meant to attack him. Most likely it was just going down the wood for better shelter and had made a feint at him in passing – as much out of curiosity or playfulness as anything. He recalled the way horses menace each other when they are galloping around in a paddock.

The wood rose to a steep bank topped by the hawthorn hedge that ran along the whole ridge of the hill. He was pulling himself up to a thin place in the hedge by the bare stem of one of the hawthorns when he ducked and shrank down again. The swelling gradient of fields lay in front of him, smoking in the slowly crossing rain. Out in the middle of the first field, tall as a statue, and a ghostly silver in the under-cloud light, stood the horse, watching the wood.

He lowered his head slowly, slithered back down the bank and crouched. An awful feeling of helplessness came over him. He felt certain the horse had been looking straight at him. Waiting for him? Was it clairvoyant?[1] Maybe a mad animal can be clairvoyant. At the same time he was ashamed to find himself acting so inanely, ducking and creeping about in this way just to keep out of sight of a horse. He tried to imagine how anybody in their senses would just walk off home. This cooled him a little, and he retreated farther down the wood. He would go back the way he had come, along under the hill crest, without any more nonsense.

The wood hummed and the rain was a cold weight, but he observed this rather than felt it. The water ran down inside his clothes and squelched in his shoes as he eased his way carefully over the bedded twigs and leaves. At every instant he expected to see the prick-eared black head looking down at him from the hedge above.

At the woodside he paused, close against a tree. The success of this last manoeuvre was restoring his confidence, but he didn't want to venture out into the open field without making sure that the horse was just where he had left it. The perfect move would be to withdraw quietly and leave the horse standing out there in the rain. He crept up again among the trees to the crest and peeped through the hedge.

The grey field and the whole slope were empty. He searched the distance. The horse was quite likely to have forgotten him altogether and wandered off. Then he raised himself and leaned out to see if it had come in close to the hedge. Before he was

[1] *Clairvoyant:* able to see things which are hidden from other people.

aware of anything the ground shook. He twisted around wildly to see how he had been caught. The black shape was above him, right across the light. Its whinnying snort and the spattering whack of its hooves seemed to be actually inside his head as he fell backwards down the bank, and leapt again like a madman, dodging among the oaks, imagining how the buffet would come and how he would be knocked headlong. Half-way down the wood the oaks gave way to bracken and old roots and stony rabbit diggings. He was well out into the middle of this before he realized he was running alone.

Gasping for breath now and cursing mechanically, without a thought for his suit he sat down on the ground to rest his shaking legs, letting the rain plaster the hair down over his forehead and watching the dense flashing lines disappear abruptly into the soil all around him as if he were watching through thick plate glass. He took deep breaths in the effort to steady his heart and regain control of himself. His right trouser turn-up was ripped at the seam and his suit jacket was splashed with the yellow mud of the top field.

Obviously the horse had been farther along the hedge above the steep field, waiting for him to come out at the woodside just as he had intended. He must have peeped through the hedge – peeping the wrong way – within yards of it.

However, this last attack had cleared up one thing. He need no longer act like a fool out of mere uncertainty as to whether the horse was simply being playful or not. It was definitely after him.

TED HUGHES: 'The Rain Horse' (from *Wodwo*)

Questions
Why did the young man think the behaviour of the Rain Horse was different from the normal behaviour of 'a horse sheltering from the rain'?
Apart from his concern about the horse, was the young man worried about anything else?
How did he prepare to defend himself?
What convinced him that the horse was not 'simply being playful'?
Do you think he needed to be ashamed of his reactions?

Discussion

How real is the Rain Horse? (Does the writing help you to believe in it? Are there any parts of the story that particularly show an increasing fear in the young man? Has the weather got anything to do with it?)

Writing

Describe a further episode in this story. Begin: 'Now he noticed that the sky had grown much darker. The rain was heavier every second, pressing down as if the earth had to be flooded before nightfall. The oaks ahead blurred and the ground drummed. He began to run. And as he ran he heard a deeper sound running with him. . . .'

It was a brave thing to do

Harold's Leap

Harold, are you asleep?
Harold, I remember your leap,
It may have killed you
But it was a brave thing to do.
Two promontories ran high into the sky,
He leapt from one rock to the other
And fell to the sea's smother.
Harold was always afraid to climb high,
But something urged him on,
He felt he should try.
I would not say that he was wrong,
Although he succeeded in doing
   nothing but die.
Would you?
Ever after that steep
Place was called Harold's Leap.
It was a brave thing to do.

STEVIE SMITH

Question
What would *you* say about Harold?

Writing
Write the poem again, but in your version invent something
which makes Harold change his mind, so that he does not die.

Beowulf braves the Dragon

Beowulf made his last brave speech: 'I fought frequently as a young man, and I will fight now in my old age to protect my people. I would scorn a sword or any weapon against the Worm if I knew how to come to grips with the grim beast, as I once did long ago with Grendel. But here I must be prepared for penetrating flames, fire and poison. Therefore I am armed with both shield and corselet. I shall not budge an inch before the guardian of that hoard. But fate will decide the issue between us on the mound. I am steeled for the encounter, and shall say no more about the doom of the Dragon.

'Watch from the hill, soldiers, which of the two of us has the greater stamina after the strife. This is not your battle, nor is it any other man's duty but my own to fight this Dragon for high honours. By my own endeavour I will end the Dragon and gain the gold; or the fight will finish your friend and King.'

Beowulf helped himself up with his shield; steadfastly, in helmet and armour, he approached the rocky cliffs, self-reliant and alone. He was no coward. Then that brave man, who had come through so many adventures and battles, saw from the top of the mound great tongues of tearing flame belching forth. No man could fight that flood of flame without being roasted alive.

Then Beowulf, full of fury, bellowed out a challenge through the cavern. Hate kindled hate. The guardian of the hoard had recognized the voice of a man. The time was past for parley. First the rocks ricocheted the fiery flame of the monster, his burning breath and hissing battle sweat. The din was tremendous. Beowulf, at the entrance, lifted his shield in front of the flames. The reptile flew at his foe. Beowulf drew his sharp ancient sword. At loggerheads, each was aware of the other's fearfulness. Beowulf took up his stance behind his shield.

The Dragon coiled himself up. Beowulf waited in his armour. The Dragon snaked at him, in folds of fire – dashing to its doom. The King's shield did not last as a protection as long as he had hoped if he was to survive that day's contest. But fate did not decree thus. Beowulf raised his sword, and struck the shimmering snake. But his bright blade glanced off the shining scales and barely bit as far home as the warrior had need if he was to survive the fray. The blow only served to enrage the ghastly guardian of the barrow, so that he spurted forth furious flames and hostile hot fire in every direction. The great ancestral sword which had served Beowulf well in times of yore betrayed him. This time there were to be no songs of victory. It was not easy for Beowulf to face the terrible journey through death, although it is a journey we all must make. Life is not for ever on this earth.

Then the contestants came at it again. The Dragon with renewed confidence summoned up great reserves of fire from his flame-hurling body. Beowulf, ruler of his people, suffered sorely from the burning of the fire. His comrades did not leap to his defence to surround him, but retreated to the shelter of the forest in fear for their own skins. But one man among them was deeply dismayed. An honest man knows where his duties lie.

Wiglaf, a companion prince, saw how sorely Beowulf suffered under the scorching armour. He remembered the favours Beowulf had bestowed on him in times gone by. There was no more thinking. Straightway he seized his yellow linden shield and lifted up his ancient sword, forged by the giants of old. This was the first time young Wiglaf was to stand by his lord in battle. His courage did not falter and his ancestral sword did not play him false, as the Dragon discovered when they met.

Sadly Wiglaf chided his companions: 'I remember that in better days when we drank mead in our lord's hall and he gave us treasures and armour, we pledged our support if ever he should be in need. He selected us especially to accompany him to this dread combat, although he chose to bear the brunt and win the victory himself alone. Now is the hour when Beowulf needs us most. Let us ignore the gnashing flames of the fire and hasten to his help. If flames are to consume him then they can have me also. Surely we cannot carry home our weapons with honour if we have not first felled the fiery foe and borne our arms bravely by our lord's side.

'It should not be his lot to be rewarded for his past bravery with solitary death at the Dragon's door. Let us make it a common lot, and with him share the strife.'

So saying, Wiglaf dared the deadly reek, and darted to the defence of his prince, urging him thus: 'Beloved Beowulf, remember the promise of your youth, that so long as you drew breath you would keep your glory bright. Do now protect your life with all your might, and I will join my strength with yours.'

No sooner had he spoken than the Dragon again sallied forth, spitting and spouting gouts of flame at his human foes. Wiglaf's shield disintegrated in the furnace of flame, and his corselet gave him no protection. But he managed to slip behind Beowulf's shield when his own dissolved in smouldering cinders. Beowulf then summoned his old valour. With a superhuman effort he crashed down his great sword, Naegling, into the Serpent's head. The ancient grey sword shattered to smithereens. It failed him in the fearful fray. Once again he was let down by his weapon. The force of his blows were so great that no weapons could withstand them. Even ancient heirlooms, trusted and tried and hardened by the blood of battles, were to no avail.

At that moment the Dragon rushed Beowulf a third time, while he was defenceless. He jammed Beowulf's neck between his great jaws and savaged him with his fangs. Beowulf was bathed in his own life-blood; the gore pulsed out in torrents. The legend runs in his country that Wiglaf straightway leapt to his hero's aid. Avoiding the head, though burned in the attempt, he stabbed his gleaming sword through the Dragon's throat, and at once the fire was dampened. Then Beowulf, summoning up his senses, drew his sharp battle-knife from his belt and ripped open the Serpent's stomach. Together, as companions, Beowulf and Wiglaf had done for the Dragon. So should dark days call forth comradely acts of courage.

Beowulf had claimed his last honour; the fever of his life was over, and his work was done.

Dictionary or Discussion
ricocheted
loggerheads

Compare the Dragon (Worm or Serpent) with Grendel. Are there any similarities? Are there any differences? (Do you think the Dragon stands for anything?)

What are the qualities of a hero that the Anglo-Saxon audience seemed to admire?

For discussion. 'The story of Beowulf is very different from that of Jack the Giant-Killer, though at first sight they have many similarities.'

Find out what you can about iron and steel. How were swords made?

Music. The Firebird by Stravinsky.

Invent a story about a twentieth-century hero defending his people against a threat to the community.

III (3) **Of songs and praises**

1. *The Terror of the Thames*
2. *I hear America Singing*
3. *It's a song about love*
4. *Praise the Lord upon earth : ye dragons and all deeps*
5. *Beowulf : of men the mildest and gentlest,*
     to his people the kindest,
     for praise the most eager

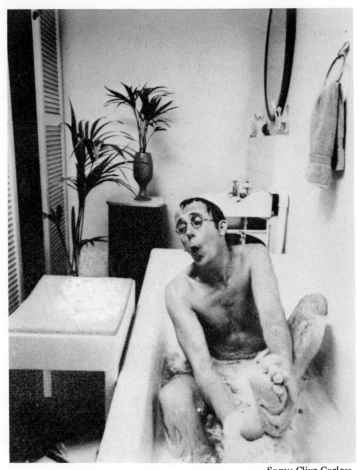

Sony: Clive Corless

Invent a story about a day in the life of the man in this picture.
Why is he singing?
Invent a song which he might be singing.
What makes *you* sing in the bath? (What makes you happy?)

The Terror of the Thames

Growltiger was a Bravo Cat, who travelled on a barge:
In fact he was the roughest cat that ever roamed at large.
From Gravesend up to Oxford he pursued his evil aims,
Rejoicing in his title of 'The Terror of the Thames'.

His manners and appearance did not calculate to please;
His coat was torn and seedy, he was baggy at the knees;
One ear was somewhat missing, no need to tell you why,
And he scowled upon a hostile world from one forbidding eye.

The cottagers of Rotherhithe knew something of his fame;
At Hammersmith and Putney people shuddered at his name.
They would fortify the hen-house, lock up the silly goose,
When the rumour ran along the shore: GROWLTIGER'S ON THE
    LOOSE!

Woe to the weak canary, that fluttered from its cage;
Woe to the pampered Pekinese, that faced Growltiger's rage;
Woe to the bristly Bandicoot, that lurks on foreign ships,
And woe to any Cat with whom Growltiger came to grips!

But most to Cats of foreign race his hatred had been vowed,
To Cats of foreign name and race no quarter was allowed.
The Persian and the Siamese regarded him with fear –
Because it was a Siamese had mauled his missing ear.

Now on a peaceful summer night, all nature seemed at play,
The tender moon was shining bright, the barge at Molesey lay.
All in the balmy moonlight it lay rocking on the tide –
And Growltiger was disposed to show his sentimental side.

His bucko mate, GRUMBUSKIN, long since had disappeared,
For to the Bell at Hampton he had gone to wet his beard;
And his bosun, TUMBLEBRUTUS, he too had stol'n away –
In the yard behind the Lion he was prowling for his prey.

In the forepeak of the vessel Growltiger sate alone,
Concentrating his attention on the Lady GRIDDLEBONE.
And his raffish crew were sleeping in their barrels and their
    bunks –
As the Siamese came creeping in their sampans and their junks.

Growltiger had no eye or ear for aught but Griddlebone,
And the Lady seemed enraptured by his manly baritone,
Disposed to relaxation, and awaiting no surprise –
But the moonlight shone reflected from a thousand bright blue
    eyes.

And closer still and closer the sampans circled round,
And yet from all the enemy there was not heard a sound.
The lovers sang their last duet, in danger of their lives –
For the foe was armed with toasting forks and cruel carving
    knives.

Then GILBERT gave the signal to his fierce Mongolian horde;
With a frightful burst of fireworks the Chinks they swarmed
    aboard.
Abandoning their sampans, and their pullaways and junks,
They battened down the hatches on the crew within their bunks.

Then Griddlebone she gave a screech, for she was badly skeered;
I am sorry to admit it, but she quickly disappeared.
She probably escaped with ease, I'm sure she was not drowned –
But a serried ring of flashing steel Growltiger did surround.

The ruthless foe pressed forward, in stubborn rank on rank;
Growltiger to his vast surprise was forced to walk the plank.
He who a hundred victims had driven to that drop,
At the end of all his crimes was forced to go ker-flip, ker-flop.

Oh there was joy in Wapping when the news flew through the
    land;
At Maidenhead and Henley there was dancing on the strand.
Rats were roasted whole at Brentford, and at Victoria Dock,
And a day of celebration was commanded in Bangkok.

T. S. ELIOT: 'Growltiger's Last Stand'

Writing

Write a poem entitled 'The Return of Growltiger'.

Write a radio commentary on Growltiger's arrival at Hammersmith and Putney. Try to create an atmosphere of fright and excitement.

(Can you make it like a commentary on the Oxford/Cambridge boat race?)

Record

If you enjoyed your encounter with Growltiger you might like to meet some more of T. S. Eliot's cats on the record *Old Possum's Book of Practical Cats* (Argo, RG 116).

I hear America singing

I hear America singing, the varied carols I hear.
Those of mechanics, each one singing his as it should be blithe
    and strong,
The carpenter singing his as he measures his plank or beam,
The mason singing his as he makes ready for work, or leaves off
    work,
The boatman singing what belongs to him in his boat, the deck-
    hand singing on the steamboat deck,
The shoemaker singing as he sits on his bench, the hatter singing
    as he stands,
The wood-cutter's song, the ploughboy's on his way in the
    morning, or at noon intermission or at sundown,
The delicious singing of the mother, or of the young wife at work,
    or of the girl sewing or washing,
Each singing what belongs to him or her and to none else,
The day what belongs to the day – at night the party of young
    fellows, robust, friendly,
Singing with open mouths their strong melodious songs.

WALT WHITMAN

Write a poem called 'I Hear England Singing'.
If you wish, substitute the name of another country.

It's a song about love

If I had a hammer,
I'd hammer in the morning,
I'd hammer in the evening,
All over this land;
I'd hammer out danger,
I'd hammer out a warning,
I'd hammer out love between all of my brothers,
All over this land.

If I had a bell,
I'd ring it in the morning,
I'd ring it in the evening,
All over this land;
I'd ring out danger,
I'd ring out a warning,
I'd ring out love between all of my brothers,
All over this land.

If I had a song,
I'd sing it in the morning,
I'd sing it in the evening,
All over this land;
I'd sing out danger,
I'd sing out a warning,
I'd sing out love between all of my brothers,
All over this land.

Well, I've got a hammer,
And I've got a bell,
And I've got a song to sing
All over this land;
It's a hammer of justice,
It's a bell of freedom,
It's a song about love between all of my brothers,
All over this land.

LEE HAYS AND PETE SEEGER: 'If I had a Hammer'

Writing
Write your own poem or song about justice, freedom and love.
Not everyone likes this song. Can you suggest why?

253

Praise the Lord upon earth: ye dragons and all deeps

O praise the Lord of heaven: praise him in the height.

Praise him, all ye angels of his: praise him, all his host.

Praise him, sun and moon: praise him, all ye stars and light.

Praise him, all ye heavens: and ye waters that are above the heavens.

Let them praise the Name of the Lord: for he spake the word, and they were made; he commanded, and they were created.

He hath made them fast for ever and ever: he hath given them a law which shall not be broken.

Praise the Lord upon earth: ye dragons, and all deeps;

Fire and hail, snow and vapours: wind and storm, fulfilling his word;

Mountains and all hills: fruitful trees and all cedars;

Beasts and all cattle: worms and feathered fowls;

Kings of the earth and all people: princes and all judges of the world;

Young men and maidens, old men and children, praise the Name of the Lord: for his Name only is excellent, and his praise above heaven and earth.

He shall exalt the horn of his people; all his saints shall praise him: even the children of Israel, even the people that serveth him.

PSALM 148

O praise God in his holiness: praise him in the firmament of his power.

Praise him in his noble acts: praise him according to his excellent greatness.

Praise him in the sound of the trumpet: praise him upon the lute and harp.

Praise him in the cymbals and dances: praise him upon the strings and pipe.

Praise him upon the well-tuned cymbals: praise him upon the loud cymbals.

Let every thing that hath breath praise the Lord.

PSALM 150

Questions
Who does the psalmist say should praise the Lord?
How should they praise the Lord?
Why should they praise the Lord?

Project
Find out as much as you can about the Psalms and the Old Testament.
Find out about holy books other than the Bible.
Make a list of some of the religions in the world, and see what they have in common, and where they differ. (You could make an illustrated book called 'The Religions of the World'.)

British Museum

Write a story or description or account of your thoughts or whatever you feel as you look at this picture.

Do you believe dragons existed?

Imagine the time when the creature in this photo was alive. Invent a story involving it. You can put yourself in the story if you wish.

Imagine that the Loch Ness monster is at last discovered. Write the newspaper report about its discovery.

Then the wound that the Dragon had dealt Beowulf earlier began to burn and swell; he soon discovered that the vile venom within him was rapidly poisoning his whole system. The King made his way to a seat by the rampart, racked with deep thought. He gazed at the work of the giants, and he saw how the ancient mouth of the mound and the vaulted roof were supported by stout pillars. The good Wiglaf bathed Beowulf's wounds with water and unloosed his helmet, as he rested, exhausted and drenched with blood.

Beowulf spoke through the pain of his wound. He knew that he had used up the time allotted him on this earth, happy days were at an end, death was fast approaching: 'I would now have wished to pass on my armour to a son, if I had been blessed with an heir to inherit it. For fifty winters have I ruled this people, unmolested and unfrightened of attacks by adjacent tribes. On earth I have patiently borne what life brought, looked after my inheritance, kept peace where I could and honoured my promises. This comforts me in my plight, because when life leaves me God cannot challenge me with the murder of my folk. Now, dear Wiglaf, go quickly and search out the treasure hoard under the grey rock, now while the Dragon is laid low, sleeping with death's wound, bereft of his treasure. Make haste, so that I might have knowledge of the old riches, the golden store, see for myself the gems and precious jewels, after which I might settle myself to quitting this life peacefully, and also the people I have looked after for so long.'

As soon as Wiglaf had heard his wounded lord's wishes, without delay, he went in his armour into the jaws of the vault. Battle-happy, he went through the entrance and beheld a host of singular treasures, shining gold littering the ground, wonders on the wall, and the den of the Worm, the dusk-flying Dragon. There were deserted drinking-cups, old goblets, abandoned and uncared for. There were many helmets, old and rusty, many bracelets skilfully wrought. Buried treasures of gold can over-throw any man. Let him hide it who will!

Wiglaf also saw, high above the treasure hoard, a solid gold standard, the finest of handwork, a tribute to man's craft. The standard reflected bright light onto the floor and the precious works of art. There was no sign of the Serpent to be seen. The sword had carried him off.

Thus, the legend goes, did one man alone rifle all the treasure hoard under the hill, the work of the giants of old. He stuffed his bosom with goblets and dishes as he saw best. He snatched up for good measure the standard, brightest of banners. The old King's iron weapon had seen off him who had guarded the treasure for a long while, protecting it by spouting fire and flame through the watches of the night until he was dealt his death blow.

Wiglaf made haste, hurrying with his treasure, eager to get back with his booty and anxious for the life of his dear prince whom he had left near to death outside the entrance. Loaded with riches, he came on Beowulf bleeding the last dregs of his life-blood. Wiglaf again revived him with water, until from his dying lips the hero whispered as he beheld the bright gold: 'I give thanks to the Prince, the King of Glory, the everlasting Lord, for the treasures that I look upon, that I have been granted to win for my people before my death-day. Now that I have bought the treasure hoard with the remains of my life, take care of my kinsmen. I cannot dally here longer. Ask the war heroes to build a resplendent tomb for me after the funeral fire, on the sea's headland. Raise it high on Hronesness, as a memorial for my people, so that sea travellers who steer their tall ships far over the salt seas shall henceforth christen it "Beowulf's Barrow".'

Then the brave Beowulf took the golden collar from his neck and gave it to young Wiglaf together with his golden helmet, ring and corselet, bidding him make good use of them: 'You are the last survivor of our family. Fate has swept all my brave kinsmen away to their destiny, and I must needs follow them.'

Those were the great man's last words before his dead body was given to the fierce flames of the funeral pyre. His soul left his body to seek the reward of the just.

Wiglaf was sorrowful to see his beloved lord at his life's end, in such wretched suffering. His slayer also lay there on the earth, the dire cave Dragon, dead and destroyed. The twisted Worm would no longer lord it over the treasure hoard, but edges of iron, hard and hacked about in battle had harried him out of his life. The far-flying Dragon had dropped dead from his wounds close to his treasure house. His night growling and his attacks from the sky were at an end, his pride in his possessions over. On earth he fell at the hand of the King. No other man, however bold, had dared face the Dragon while he watched over his hoard. Beowulf now had paid for the treasures with his life. Together they ended their transient days.

Soon the traitors crept out of the wood, ten cowards together, who lacked the courage to lift their spears at the moment of their lord's great need. In shame they bore their shields to where the King lay. They regarded Wiglaf. He sat, exhausted, by Beowulf's shoulders, attempting in vain to revive him with water. Much as he wanted, he could not keep Beowulf alive longer. All men's destinies, both high and low, are in the lap of the Lord.

Wiglaf bitterly reproached the cowardice of the men whose sight he could scarce bear: 'Beowulf squandered in vain his gifts of armour on you. When the time of need came, you failed him. One was too few to save his life. Now the giving of jewels, receiving of swords, the enjoyment of your own hearth and happiness is over for you and yours. You are doomed to a life of wandering, deprived of all possessions, as soon as the news of your flight and fear reaches the ears of princes far and wide. Death is better to a warrior than a life of reproach.'

Then Wiglaf ordered a messenger to relate the tidings to the warriors waiting on the sea cliff, where all the long morning they had anxiously waited to hear whether Beowulf had defeated the Dragon or died in the attempt. The messenger was quick to blurt out the news: 'Beowulf is dead of the Dragon. The Dragon also lies dead by his side, prey of Beowulf's dagger after his sword had failed. Wiglaf, weary with sorrow, kept vigil over the bodies of friend and foe. Now it is likely that there will be wars, as soon as the news of the King's death reaches our enemies. It was Beowulf who kept them off in the past, protected our wealth and our kingdom, and looked to his people's welfare in addition to performing brave deeds.

'Let us make haste to see the King and bear him on his way to his funeral pyre. Every piece of the treasure he dearly bought with his life shall burn with him. No man will wear a precious memento. No fair maiden will wear a priceless necklace. Deprived of gold and downcast in spirits they shall time and time again tread the paths of exile, now that the hero has done with laughter, joy and merriment. From now on, in the chill of morning many a spear will be clutched for with the fingers, and grasped in the hand. The sound of the harp will not wake the warriors, but the black raven, impatient for its prey, shall recount many things, and boast to the eagle how he banqueted at the feast, when he shared the spoils of the dead with the wolf.'

Thus the messenger told his news, and he was not far wrong in his prophecies.

Then they all got up and sadly wended their way to Eagles' Ness to see the sorry sight. They beheld dear Beowulf dead, and the hateful Serpent hard by. The Fire-Dragon, terrible in its mottled colouring, scorched with the flames, measured fifty feet long where it lay. Its free-flying days were over. It was bound stiffly by death. No more would it make a home in an earth cave. Goblets and flagons stood by it, dishes and costly swords rusted there as though they had been decaying for a thousand winters buried in the bosom of the earth. The golden treasure of old had been under a spell, until God had seen fit to allow the hero of his choice to break it.

Wiglaf addressed the warriors: 'Now the hoard can be seen by all, bought at a terrible price. The old King in his final moments asked me to greet you, and he bade you build a memorial on the site of his funeral pyre, a barrow befitting his rank and fame. Come now, and I will visit again as your guide the treasures within the tumulus, so that you may behold the rings and rich gold for yourselves. Meanwhile let the bier be prepared, so that when we come out we can carry Beowulf to his cremation and the keeping of the Almighty.'

Then Wiglaf gave orders for wood to be fetched for the funeral fire from far and wide. He chose seven of the King's men, one bearing a flaming brand, to light the way into the Dragon's den. Nothing was ordered by lot. They all carried off what they could. They pushed the Dragon, the Worm, the guardian of the treasures, over the cliff edge, made the brimming seas his burial place. A wagon was loaded with a priceless pile of twisted gold. Prince Beowulf was borne away to Hronesness.

There the people made for him, as he had asked, a splendid funeral pyre, hung round with helmets, battle-shields and bright corselets. Then the warriors, mourning, laid in the midst their beloved lord, Beowulf. They began to set fire to the mountainous funeral pyre. The swirl of wood smoke shot up like a fountain, black above the red fire; the crackling of the flames was confused with the cries of sorrow, until with the dropping of the wind the bones crumbled into hot ashes. Downcast and depressed they lamented their lord's death. His kinswoman, her hair bound up, keened a dirge in Beowulf's memory, prophesying again and again the hard times that were sure to follow, with bloodshed, fire and sword, rack and ruin. Heaven swallowed up the smoke.

Then Beowulf's kinsmen built a barrow on the cliff, high and broad and visible far and wide to voyagers over the seas. In ten days they had completed the building of brave Beowulf's Beacon. Round his ashes they erected the finest tomb the architects could devise. In the barrow they buried collars and brooches, and all the adornments that had been plundered from the treasure hoard. They left the ancient gold in the safe keeping of the earth, where it lies to this day, as useless to men as it was before.

Then twelve warriors rode round the barrow and sang the praises of Beowulf. They praised his manhood, they praised his heroism, they praised him as men should praise their king when his time comes. This is how Beowulf's kinsmen praised him. They said that he was of worldly kings the mildest, and of men the gentlest, to his people the kindest, and for glory the most eager.

Dictionary or Discussion
   adjacent
   singular (in the sense of 'extraordinary')
   resplendent
   by lot

Imagine you are Wiglaf. Relate to a comrade why you went into the cave, what you saw, and Beowulf's last thoughts and wishes.

Write a memorial poem for Beowulf.

Find out about serpents in England. (Where do you find them? Which are poisonous? How do you recognize them? What can be done about venomous serpent stings?)

What do you think the Anglo-Saxon audience enjoyed about the story of Beowulf? What did you enjoy most about it?

Plan an expedition to excavate Beowulf's Barrow. (Where will you look for it? What will you take with you? Would you expect to find any unusual difficulties, even if you discovered the Barrow? Could it still be under a spell?)

Write the praises of any twentieth-century hero.

When and how did Christianity come to Britain? What was here before?

Imagine that a monk found the Beowulf story, and that when he found it, it was completely without any Christian references. Discuss what parts of the story might have made him think that it was a suitable story to preserve to illustrate Christian ideas and ideals. (For example, is Beowulf a person who acts like a Christian?)

Drama. Link together the episodes you have improvised from Beowulf into a complete play, and include the death and burial of Beowulf. Write a poem or a song entitled 'In praise of Beowulf'. Use it to accompany the final scene.

Record. Some of the Beowulf story is recorded – in modern English – on Argo ZPL 1057 (stereo).

III (4) Epilogue

The Mystery

Along the avenue of cypresses,
All in their scarlet cloaks and surplices
Of linen, go the chanting choristers,
The priests in gold and black, the villagers.

And all along the path to the cemetery
The round dark heads of men crowd silently,
And black-scarved faces of womenfolk, wistfully
Watch at the banner of death, and the mystery.

And at the foot of a grave a father stands
With sunken head, and forgotten, folded hands;
And at the foot of a grave a mother kneels
With pale shut face, nor either hears nor feels

The coming of the chanting choristers
Between the avenues of cypresses,
The silence of the many villagers,
The candle-flames beside the surplices.

D. H. LAWRENCE: *Giorno dei Morti*

My Life Story

The earliest thing I can remember doing occurred when I was four. I was staying with my grandparents, and my grandfather and father were going to the 'local' for a drink before dinner. I went with them, riding on the back of Rex, my grandad's dog, who was about three times my size. There is no real reason why this should stay in my memory, but it has.

Although I cannot remember further back than this, I do know certain things about myself. I was born in East London, where I remained until I was eleven. We lived in one of a row of identical houses, on the first floor of a three-storey house. We had three rooms, a kitchen, a back-room, and a front-room. Sometimes the back-room was the living-room, sometimes the front-room. The other room was the bedroom. Our landlady lived on the ground floor, and I was in constant fear lest I incurred her wrath by making a noise. To get to the garden, we had to go through her passage, which she disliked, with the result that I played in the street rather than in the garden, which was overgrown with weeds, anyway.

Every day, the factories around us poured clouds of grey-black smoke onto us. This, combined with games which involved crawling through hedges and over walls, made the children in our street usually look dirty, and, according to my father, I was the dirtiest of them all. He said there was never a day when he came home to find me not smeared with dirt and grime, with my hair hanging loose, and my frock torn.

Although I had plenty of friends, I spent a lot of time on my own. I had a number of dolls, including Peggy-Lil, an enormous baby-doll. I also had an imaginary friend, called Doris, who lived behind the gas-stove, and always managed to be sitting on a chair when one of my parents wanted to sit on it.

I am told that I took an almost maniacal delight in piling up empty jam-jars behind the kitchen-door, and seeing somebody open the door and knock everything over.

In bed at night I used to make up plays about my dolls, and fairy-tale characters, and myself, taking all the parts, and talking out loud. At four-and-a-half, I joined school. It was not a modern school, in fact, it will be a century old next year. There are traces of an old arch over one of the doors, and a bell-tower without a bell, relics of a time when the building was a monastic school.

I must have been a real problem for some of my earlier teachers. I did not learn to read until fairly late in schooling, in spite of the hours spent with my mother in front of the fire, trying to learn my alphabet. For at least eighteen months I could count only as far as five before I became stuck. But by the time I had reached the top infant class I and my friends were sitting out most of the lessons, already knowing them. This, as can be imagined, made us very proud, so that the sudden bump into reality was all the more noticeable when I entered the junior part of the school. In my second year in the juniors, I went completely haywire. I dawdled purposely on the way to school; I did not worry much about attending to lessons; I just did not care.

By this time I was leader of a small clique of children, Jeanie, Jacqueline, Maureen, Pamela, and Brenda. Jeanie was, at the time, my best friend, in spite of the fact that we quarrelled incessantly. There was always a certain amount of rivalry between us, too. When playing a game, we always tried to put over our own ideas, rather than follow the other's lead. Because of this, the games became very much Jeanie's and mine, with the others just doing as they were told. I still made up stories at night, and sometimes during the day, but now I was the proprietress of a hotel. Our bedroom, then in the front-room, became a dormitory. The living-room was the lounge. The kitchen I split into three strips. The strip where the table was, was the dining-room, the strip with the gas-stove, the kitchen, and the part with the sink, the bath-room. The road outside was a river, and road-vehicles were sailing-craft. Behind a panel in the wall I kept a horse, and a dog slept under my bed.

When I was seven, my sister was born. Julie was, and is, as different to me as can be possible. She hated animals, whereas I loved them. This is odd, because although Julie has never been frightened by an animal, I, at the age of three, was knocked down by an enormous Alsatian dog.

Julie is rarely sentimental, whereas I, at four, was crying over the plight of Sammy the Seal on a Children's Hour Programme on the radio. I still cry over sad books and films, because the characters become so real to me. In the same way, I become angry, or happy, or puzzled, as the characters do. I often feel a savage satisfaction when a particularly villainous villain is overcome, although I usually dislike violence on television or films, even if the hero is unhurt.

As I have said, I was a slow starter at school, but Julie knew her alphabet, could write her name, and count up to a hundred, all before she even started school. Now, after being at school for less than two years, she reads excellently. In fact, our love of books is about the only thing Julie and I share.

As well as being intelligent, Julie is pretty and practical. This last is really a good thing, as my mother needs at least one daughter who knows how to cook and sew properly, as Julie will soon do, and I'm certainly no use to her in this direction.

But this practicalness just adds to the list of differences between us, so that I and my sister really circulate in two different spheres, our only point of contact being the fact that we share the same parents, house, and room.

As I said, during my second year in the junior part of school, I went mad, but in the third year I settled down again. My greatest delight, during the next two years, was the talks I had with my teacher, a man, after morning school, before I went to dinner. We talked about anything and everything. When, during the fourth year, my teacher had to take a course in some subject, and we had a new teacher for a while, I thought I would have to give up my talks, but, to my delight, I found I could talk just as easily to the new teacher.

In the fourth year, I only had one real friend, Jackie. Pamela had moved, and Jeanie, Maureen, and Brenda all did their third-year twice, being a few weeks too young to take the 'Eleven-Plus' examination with the rest of us. Also, Jeanie and I had had two bad quarrels, and after that we were never terribly friendly with one another.

At the beginning of the fourth year, I took the 'Eleven-Plus'. I had none of the fears about this that the books say we all have, nor for that matter, did anybody else in my class. I think that this was largely due to our teacher, who explained that this was not a competition, but an assessment.

After the examination, things seemed very slack. It was rather like a long, boring holiday. Talking of holidays, my favourite were those spent in the little village in Northampton where my grandparents live. The fields of corn, the pastures, the funny little streets, the way everybody knew everybody else, all combined to fascinate me as a small child, and I was firm in my ambition to buy a cottage out there. But as I grew older, I found drawbacks. There was a cinema, but nothing else to amuse me. Although all my mother's relations lived there, and all had children, all my cousins were younger than I, the nearest being a boy two years younger. And the adults were continually drawing me into the intricate web of gossip which must spring up whenever a whole family, including in-laws, live within a few streets of one another.

As well as summer holidays there, we went to the village every other year, for Christmas. All the family crowded into my grandmother's small house, and the adults would eat and drink and talk, while the children, usually supervised by me, played in the 'shop' in the front of the house. Actually, my cousins did not mind me 'lording it' over them, because I was 'from London', and that made all the difference. But of course, we did not only go to Northampton for holidays. Every year we went to the sea as well. One year we stayed in a bungalow. Behind the bungalow was a very shallow stream, scarcely half-an-inch deep, which everybody crossed by means of a wooden plank. One day I decided to find out why people could not walk across the stream. Unfortunately, the bed of the stream was very soft mud. I had sunk up to my shins before anybody spotted my predicament.

Another year we stayed in a caravan. My parents swear they will never do it again. Every time my father went through the door he hit his head against the top of it. It rained every night, and an apple-tree outside the caravan invariably dripped water onto the iron roof. Because of the lack of room, Julie and I ate our meals on a collapsible table outside, and one day the legs of the table at my end collapsed, and the bacon and eggs which I had intended to eat for breakfast cascaded onto my lap and the grass. But there were lighter moments. For instance, when I dressed Julie up as a boy, by tucking her hair into a cotton cap and dressing her in shorts, and she announced herself to the people in the next caravan as 'Jimmy, Julie's twin brother'. They believed it, too, and by constantly changing Julie's identity, we fooled them right up to the last day, when we enlightened them.

To return to the last year at primary school. The time dragged by. At last, the results came through. I was to go to a grammar school. The school I went to was only about a hundred yards from where I lived. Two years before I joined, the school had celebrated its Jubilee Year. Ever since I was a small child I had dreamed of attending this school.

During the summer holiday before I started at this school, I nearly went mad with boredom. About half-way through I suddenly contracted an unknown illness. I privately decided that I had poliomyelitis. A vivid imagination can be a handicap. As a little girl I lived in constant fear of a wolf entering the house. Whenever I was on my own I use to sit at the kitchen-table, staring out of the window, so that if a wolf did come through the door I would not see it. The same imagination which had made every sound into a wolf's footfall now turned every ache into approaching paralysis.

But once term started, all my worries cleared up. I was very happy at that school, but I had scarcely been there a term-and-a-half when we were offered a flat in Blackheath Village, and my parents accepted it.

The Friday I left my first school I had no idea where I was to go next. The next Monday I was installed at Kidbrooke Comprehensive School. Until then, neither my parents nor I had ever heard of Kidbrooke. If it came to that, we had never even heard of Blackheath. It could have been the other side of the world for all we knew of it. But when we settled down, we were all delighted with our new surroundings. I liked my new school, although the size of it bewildered me – I was ten minutes late for two lessons in the first week because I lost myself. Eventually I became used to the maze of corridors, stairs, and floors, and now I find it extremely amusing to see first-formers wandering around in the same predicament as I was once in.

About eighteen months ago I suddenly discovered that I liked popular songs and musicians. I started a scrap-book, which, of course, entailed 'wasting' my money on pictures to put into it. Although we had had television ever since Julie was born, we only had one channel, and when we recently bought a television with two, I was suddenly plunged into a world where Westerns abounded. This had a pronounced effect on the stories which I still make up at night. Now, they are about popular singers and television Western heroes, and I do not figure in them at all.

So here I am. At thirteen, not so very different from when I was three, or any other age. I still tell myself stories, even if they have changed in character. I still cry at sad films. I still read books almost indiscriminately. I still spend a lot of time alone. I still enjoy school. I still try to impress my ideas on others. At seven, I was going to be an authoress. Although, since then, I have wanted to be an advertiser, a producer, and an actress, it has always been connected with words.

Now I would like to be a journalist, and I still want, very much, to write a book, although I do not think I have the perseverance. But one can day-dream, and having day-dreamed since I was an infant, I doubt very much if I shall give it up now.

ANGELA IRENE STRATTON, 13

(Award–winning entry, *Daily Mirror* Children's Literary Competition)

Questions

'But one can day-dream, and having day-dreamed since I was an infant, I doubt very much if I shall give it up now.' – What were Angela's day-dreams?

'I still want, very much, to write a book.' – Can you find any clues which seem to show that Angela had the beginnings of a writer in her from a very early age? What qualities and person-ality do you think a writer should have? What quality does Angela think she lacks, which might prevent her from becoming a successful writer?

Explain what Angela means by:

'an almost maniacal delight'

'relics of a time when the building was a monastic school'

'the sudden bump into reality'

'a small clique'

'I went completely haywire'

'Julie is rarely sentimental'

'I and my sister really circulate in two different spheres'

'I found drawbacks'

'And the adults were continually drawing me into the intricate web of gossip which must spring up whenever a whole family, including in-laws, live within a few streets of one another'

'my cousins did not mind me "lording it" over them, because I was "from London", and that made all the difference'

'before anybody spotted my predicament'

'by constantly changing Julie's identity, we fooled them right up to the last day, when we enlightened them' 'the same imagination which had made every sound into a wolf's footfall now turned every ache into approaching paralysis'

'This had a pronounced effect on the stories which I still make up at night'

'I still read books almost indiscriminately'.

Discussion

Discuss the merits you think the judges of the writing competition found in Angela's 'Life Story'. Do you find anything in the writing which you don't like?

Divide into imaginary family groups of five or six. Imagine that the family have saved £100 for a holiday. Discuss the kind of holiday you want to take, the place, the time, the accommodation, method of travel, ways of saving extra funds if necessary, and anything else you consider important. You might wish to send away for or collect relevant brochures or details from travel agents, or from newspaper advertisements.

Improvisation

'An episode in a caravan holiday.'

Project

Find out all you can about 'Literary Competitions'. What is their purpose? Are there arguments both for and against them? Find out about the *Daily Mirror* Children's Literary Competition. When is it held? Who judges it? What do the judges look for in the writing? What books have won adult literary competitions? Have any books written particularly for 12/13-year-olds won any awards?

Organize a literary competition. How far will it extend? Who will judge it?

Make plans to enter the next *Daily Mirror* Competition.

Writing

'*My* Life Story.'

Further reading

The Lark in the Morn by Elfrida Vipont (Oxford Children's Library).

The Lark on the Wing by Elfrida Vipont (Oxford Children's Library).

(This book won the Carnegie medal for the outstanding book of 1950.)

If you like the first two, you might like to go on to:

The Spring of the Year and *Flowering Spring*, which continue the family story.

J. Allan Cash

What does this picture suggest to you? Write a story or description or account of your thoughts or whatever you feel or imagine as you look at it.
A famous artist said that his first memory was being brought to see this view. What are *your* earliest memories?

Make me content

Words

Out of us all
That make rhymes,
Will you choose
Sometimes –
As the winds use
A crack in a wall
Or a drain,
Their joy or their pain
To whistle through –
Choose me,
You English words?

I know you:
You are light as dreams,
Tough as oak,
Precious as gold,
As poppies and corn,
Or an old cloak:
Sweet as our birds
To the ear,
As the burnet rose
In the heat
Of Midsummer:
Strange as the races
Of dead and unborn:
Strange and sweet
Equally,
And familiar,
To the eye,
As the dearest faces
That a man knows,
And as lost homes are:

But though older far
Than oldest yew, –

As our hills are, old, –
Worn new
Again and again:
Young as our streams
After rain:
And as dear
As the earth which you prove
That we love.

Make me content
With some sweetness
From Wales
Whose nightingales
Have no wings, –
From Wiltshire and Kent
And Herefordshire,
And the villages there, –
From the names, and the things
No less.
Let me sometimes dance
With you,
Or climb
Or stand perchance
In ecstasy,
Fixed and free
In a rhyme,
As poets do.

EDWARD THOMAS